SELF-DEVELOPMENT

— WITH

ASTROLOGY

Other titles by Sheila Geddes:

Astrology (MacDonald 'Guidelines' series)
The Art of Astrology
Astrology and Health

Sheila Geddes, D.F. Astrol. S., became a practising professional astrologer in 1965. In the 1970s she was the secretary, and later an examiner and chairman of the examining board, of the Faculty of Astrological Studies. She has appeared on many 'phone-in' programmes, answering questions on astrology in all parts of this country, and in Hong Kong, Fiji and New Zealand, and she has given seminars in the UK, Australia and New Zealand. Now retired to her native Norfolk, she devotes her time to other types of writing, gardening and country pursuits.

SELF-DEVELOPMENT

– WITH –

ASTROLOGY

– Sheila Geddes –

foulsham
London • New York • Toronto • Sydney

foulsham

Yeovil Road, Slough, Berkshire, SL1 4JH

ISBN 0–572–01534–8

Copyright © 1990 Sheila Geddes

Printed in Great Britain by Cox & Wyman Ltd, Reading, Berkshire

To the memory of John Addey, M.A., D.F. Astrol. S., A.F. Astrol. S., who wrote, 'The human will cannot be otherwise than perpetually free because it is the elective faculty of a free spiritual being.'

CONTENTS

ACKNOWLEDGEMENTS

The author and publishers wish to acknowledge permissions granted as follows:

Aquarian Press for extracts from *Synastry* by Penny Thornton, *Astrology and Health* by Sheila Geddes, *Astrological Counselling* by Christina Rose, *Relating* by Liz Greene and *What We May Be* by Piero Ferrucci.

Viking Press for extracts from *The Farther Reaches Of Human Nature* by Abraham Maslow.

The author's thanks are also due to her sister, Rosemary Langford, for typing and to her husband, Alec Geddes, for proof reading.

INTRODUCTION

Our personalities are very complex. Some of us can handle the great problems in our lives better than the small ones. Some people can be described as being their own worst enemy, and nearly all of us harm ourselves in some ways simply because we are not aware of the manner in which we habitually react to situations.

Astrology is not just a method of predicting the future, as suggested by magazine columns — indeed, that is its weakest aspect. What it can do supremely well is to reveal the personality as shown by an accurate birth chart. It follows that the interpretation of such a chart can help us to know ourselves and to overcome our limitations. (See page 159 for how to obtain your free personal birth chart.)

Although it is a complex subject, you do not need to be an astrologer to benefit from this book. Just keep in mind that the characteristics attributed to each zodiac sign are valid whether we are talking about the sun in that sign, or the moon or any of the planets, though each will refer to a different facet of the personality. You will find all this explained simply in the book.

I am inviting you to come with me on a journey of self-development, an exploration into the interior of — yourself. It will be exciting and revealing, sometimes a little scary, but very rewarding, as you learn how to overcome your difficulties and exploit your strengths.

1
HOW ASTROLOGY CAN HELP YOU

When Robert was eight years old, his mother asked me to set up his birth chart and to advise her on the type of upbringing and education which he needed.

I am always delighted when this happens, because it means that the parents appreciate that their child is an individual and that his needs will differ from those of brothers and sisters.

This attitude is becoming more common, but there are still many parents who believe that the training which they were given as children is right for everyone, or that it is their duty to fit their child for the career which they had (or would have liked), with no reference to the child's temperament or aptitudes.

In Robert's case, I was able to tell his parents that he was a boy with many interests, who must have outdoor exercise if he was to be healthy. I also suggested that he might have an above-average artistic ability — perhaps music?

Yes, his musical talents had already been recognised and they hoped he would be accepted by a school of music later on.

Two years later, Robert was accepted by two famous music schools, where he would also receive formal education. Which did I think most suitable? I advised that he needed to feel that he had a secure base and might be happier at the school where he could come home each weekend, instead of being a boarder all term. This one also had the advantage of being a school where he could swim daily. I also pointed out that Robert had a strong intuitive knowledge of what was right for himself and that his parents should let him be the judge.

He was accepted by the school I suggested and his mother wrote, "He is 100 per cent confident that this school is right."

Nothing that I told his parents was a surprise to them. They understood his character well and would probably have come to the same decision themselves. So why did they consult an astrologer? By doing so they learnt which of Robert's characteristics as a young child were likely to endure into adulthood, because they were basic to his personality. The chart also indicated the possibility of a brilliant and public career, so they knew that their efforts on his education would not be wasted. I look forward to seeing Robert as a solo violinist on the concert platform, in a few years time. (For astrologers, his birth chart is given in Appendix 1 on page 153.)

Robert is a fortunate child in two respects. Firstly, he already knows where he is going and what he wants to make of his life. Secondly, he has parents who are well aware that each child has different psychological characteristics which need to be considered.

It is not easy to be a parent, though some people take the duty lightly, while many more are unaware of their own inhibitions and prejudices and believe that everyone is much the same as themselves. The more enlightened realise that children's personalities differ enormously and that a severe reprimand to one child will have little effect unless backed up by some form of punishment, while his brother may be extremely upset by even a gentle reproach.

We are all victims, to a greater or lesser extent, of our parents' failure to help us to develop our own individuality. They are not to be blamed for this — they thought they were protecting us by insisting that we conform to 'normal' practices. Normal, that is, for the time and place in which they lived. We, in our turn, will inflict similar standards upon our own children unless we take a great deal of trouble to appreciate each one's individuality and to actively encourage it. The result of our training during the formative years — not only from parents but also from teachers or other relatives — almost always inhibits us from expressing our true selves, or even being aware of who we are. We range from the slightly inhibited to psychological cripples, in cases of parental neglect or cruelty.

The intention of this book is to show how you can realise the potential of your true personality, developing your best traits and abilities and overcoming the ones which hold you back from achieving your goals.

An understanding of yourself can help you to succeed in your chosen career, find happiness in relationships, deal with or even prevent ill health and overcome inhibitions. You will see how you are responsible for many of your own problems and limitations.

At this point, most people say, "But I do know myself and my faults." That is what I thought.

I attended an encounter group and asked for some help in dealing with a difficult client. I had described myself as a relaxed person, who worried about little and forgave myself easily for my faults. The session which followed showed that I had been blaming myself (quite unjustly) for not being able to help a lady who was determined not to be helped. I had concluded that it was my own inadequacy that was at fault and I took some convincing that it was not. Hardly the feelings of someone who didn't worry and who forgave themselves easily! That session convinced me that I did not know myself half as well as I thought I did and led me to conclude that this must be the case for most people.

If your only experience of astrology has been the so-called 'predictions' in newspapers and magazines, remember that these general forecasts, based solely on the sun sign, are hit-and-miss affairs at best. Even interpretations done by astrologers from an individual birth chart may be unsatisfactory, as they depend on the competence of the astrologer. But what astrology can do well is to reflect the unique characteristics and potentials that the subject of each birthchart has brought into existence at the time of birth. By the time adulthood is reached, these characteristics will still be true, but by that time, the individual will have modified some of the traits, as life has taught its lesson. Nevertheless, the characteristics remain valid, even though the individual may have learned to control or conceal them, or they may have been suppressed or even over-exaggerated as a result of coping with life's experiences.

Astrology is a complicated subject and I am not going to teach you to become an astrologer, but even some basic knowledge of your birth chart can give insights into your personality.

To construct a birth chart properly an astrologer needs to know the date, time and place of birth. Not everyone can supply the time and this limits the information available, but there is still enough left to be helpful, especially as you can often guess the missing information as you begin to know yourself better. The birth chart is a diagram constructed from this information of the positions of the sun, moon and planets at the time and place of birth. There are many theories, but no definite reason why the interrelationships of these positions should give any clues to character, but astrologers know that they do, often precisely.

Most people identify with many of the characteristics of their sun sign, the zodiac sign in which the sun was positioned at the time of birth. The sun's dates for each sign are as follows:

Aries	20th March to 18th April.
Taurus	19th April to 19th May.
Gemini	20th May to 20th June.
Cancer	21st June to 21st July.
Leo	22nd July to 20th August.
Virgo	21st August to 21st September.
Libra	22nd September to 22nd October.
Scorpio	23rd October to 21st November.
Sagittarius	22nd November to 20th December.
Capricorn	21st December to 19th January.
Aquarius	20th January to 18th February.
Pisces	19th February to 19th March.

☉	Sun	♃	Jupiter
☽	Moon	♄	Saturn
☿	Mercury	♅	Uranus
♀	Venus	♆	Neptune
♂	Mars	♇	Pluto

♈	Aries	♎	Libra
♉	Taurus	♏	Scorpio
♊	Gemini	♐	Sagittarius
♋	Cancer	♑	Capricorn
♌	Leo	♒	Aquarius
♍	Virgo	♓	Pisces

The dates are approximate since the sun does not move into the next sign of the zodiac at exactly the same time each year.

The position of the sun in the birth chart is interpreted as indicating the basic character and most people would recognise the characteristics given for the sun sign in themselves. However, this is only one aspect of the personality, though an important one, and some of the sun-sign traits will be modified (or even outweighed) by the positions of other planets.

Here is a brief description of the characteristics shown by each of the zodiac signs*. These are not *necessarily* qualities associated with individual personalities, but are the qualities traditionally attributed to each sign of the zodiac. You will learn more of each sign in successive chapters.

ARIES (The Ram)

This is traditionally considered to be the first sign of the zodiac, the sun moving into the part of the sky known as Aries at the time of the spring equinox. It is classed as one of the three Fire signs (the other Fire signs are Leo and Sagittarius), which are characteristically energetic, enthusiastic and positive in attitude.

Each zodiac sign is said to be 'ruled' by a planet and Aries is ruled by Mars, the planet of vitality and drive, so the Arien type is full of energy and always 'raring to go'.

Aries tends to rush into situations without thinking and is generally quick and impulsive.

Aries' courage and disregard for danger is legendary. He enjoys situations which call for quick action, initiative and leadership. Aries has a pioneering spirit and loves to start new projects, but loses interest when they are running smoothly and is quickly bored.

---

*More detailed descriptions can be found in the author's *Art of Astrology* and *Astrology and Health*. See appendix.

Aries can be pugnacious and quick-tempered, but nothing lasts long. However, words like 'patience' and 'tact' are not in the Aries vocabulary, so you will always know where you stand with the Arien, who is direct, quickwitted and performs well under pressure.

TAURUS (The Bull)

This is the first of the three Earth signs (the others are Virgo and Capricorn) which are characteristically practical, static and negative in attitude. ('Negative' in this case means inclined to introversion, although this is only relative and does not imply imbalance). Taurus is ruled by Venus, the planet of love and beauty. It is the 'earthiest' of the Earth signs, Taureans needing to feel they have their feet on the ground.

They are practical, reliable, patient and stubborn and resistant to change and will do nothing which may threaten security. In order to feel secure, Taurus tends to be acquisitive and possessive, with a flair for finance and no fear of responsibility.

The influence of Venus is shown in the Taurean love of beauty and Taurus is often a connoisseur of the good things in life and is usually a lover of nature and of the comforts of home.

The Taurean child may not learn quickly, but will retain what is learned and will be methodical.

Generally, Taurus is warm-natured and affectionate, but tends to be possessive and jealous in personal relationships.

GEMINI (The Twins)

This sign is ruled by Mercury, the planet of communication and the intellect. It is the first of the three Air signs (the others are Libra and Aquarius) which are characteristically intellectual, communicative and positive (extrovert). It is also known as an adaptable sign and 'the Twins' express the duality which is so much a part of the Geminian personality. Gemini is thoughtful, intelligent and quickwitted.

Thoughts and words matter to Gemini, who is a lively debater and communicator. Gemini often goes into careers connected with communications, though there is a dislike of routine and a need for plenty of variety, so careers are liked which require travel or freedom to plan.

Gemini can change its mind often and has little perseverance, so that there is a tendency to learn a little about a great many things and difficulty in acquiring expert knowledge in any one subject. In the same way, Gemini will start many projects with great enthusiasm, but seldom completes them.

They form good relationships with others and tend to remain close to the family, particularly to brothers and sisters, but can appear to be lacking in feelings and may strike others as cold-natured.

CANCER (The Crab)

This is the first of the Water signs (the others are Scorpio and Pisces) and it is considered to be ruled by the moon. The moon represents the feelings and emotions and Water signs are also emotional, intuitive and negative (introverted).

The moon also expresses the female side of the personality and Cancer represents the maternal nature. Cancer is protective and tenacious — both women and men with this attribute like to 'look after' their own pet projects, or take jobs where they are looking after other people in some way. Cancer enjoys nursing and nurturing, in a true maternal fashion and this sign is common in catering, hotel work, running nursing homes or children's homes, etc.

Cancer tends to be rather moody, sometimes lively and optimistic and then depressed for no apparent reason. Some people with strong Cancerian qualities seem to be directly influenced by the moon and, if this sign is prominent in your birthchart, it is worth watching the moon's phases and the effects that they produce.

As you would expect, Cancer is a good homemaker and loves families and is not happy without a home base. Like the crab, Cancer appears to be hardshelled, but is really sensitive and easily hurt.

Cancer is *the* worrier of the zodiac — often for no good reason. They have good memories and tend to be drawn to anything connected with the past, thus being attracted by history, pageantry and antiques. Cancer represents intuition, imagination and sympathy.

LEO (The Lion)

This is a Fire sign, so energy and enthusiasm are part of the Leo nature. Appropriately, its ruler is the sun and Leos are normally sunny-natured — optimistic and positive.

Leo is more practical than Aries and is better able to harness enthusiasm to worthwhile projects, and since Leo is a marvellous organiser, those exhibiting this quality are often thrust into positions of great responsibility. This will not worry Leo at all, since there is an instinctive feeling that the right place is at the top. Great personal power, and genuine affection and generosity, encourage others to accept Leo as a well-liked leader.

With a lot of pride, self-respect, dignity and great courage, Leo is able to put on a mask of well-being, even when life is not being kind.

Leo is often larger than life, with ideas on a grandiose

scale, which sometimes seem wildly extravagant. As Leo is a constructive thinker, once a project has been undertaken, however large, it will be seen through to the end.

The Leo nature is warm and affectionate, but can easily be hurt if it is not sufficiently appreciated, although Leo will hide feelings. A consummate actor, Leo can radiate confidence whether it is justified or not.

VIRGO (The Virgin)

Although the ruler of Virgo is Mercury, as it was for Gemini, this is an Earth sign, so Virgo embodies much more practicality than Gemini. The same interest in intellectual activity and communication is evident, but this is now 'down to earth' and Virgo will enjoy office routine and discipline.

The emphasis on the intellect makes Virgos interested in how things work and they will take immense trouble to find out. Virgo enjoys critical and detailed work and this can result in fussiness and an over-emphasis on getting every little thing just right.

Virgo is both self-critical and critical of others, expressed in extremely high standards (often impossibly high), with a desire for perfection. Wholesomeness in diet and a great interest in health and hygiene are also attributes of Virgo.

Usually having a great desire to serve their fellow beings, Virgo prefers to work in the background, not liking the limelight and being rather shy, tending to lack self-confidence.

However, Virgos have a good opinion (fully justified) of their own capabilities and find it difficult to delegate work preferring to do things in their own way and to exacting standards. Virgo is a hard worker and expects no less of others.

LIBRA (The Scales)

This is another Air sign, so Libra tends to be intellectually orientated and communicative like Gemini. Here the resemblance ends, as Libra is considered to be 'ruled' by Venus, the planet of relationships, so there is depth of feeling present and a need for harmonious relationships, together with the appreciation for beauty and art which Venus bestows.

The sign of the scales (or balance) shows Libra's greatest attribute, a strong sense of justice. Libra abhors unpleasantness and exhibits strong diplomatic tendencies. Equally, Libra finds it difficult to cope with unpleasant conditions and longs for life to be free from stress.

The propensity to see both sides of a question or problem (balance again) makes 'sitting on the fence' a Libran attribute.

Libra has a need to find a balance with the perfect partner and is often 'in love with love', finding that the ideal is elusive as Libra is over-quick to weigh-up the faults in other people.

However, charm of manner and the desire to make life pleasant for all ensures that Libra never lacks friends.

SCORPIO (The Scorpion and the Eagle)

The second of the Water signs embodies the emotional, intuitive and introspective attributes, here combined with practicality and caution.

Modern astrologers award the rulership of Scorpio to Pluto, the refiner and regenerator. Before the discovery of Pluto, the ruler was thought to be Mars. Both of these planets signify power and passion and certainly Scorpio is the most intense of the zodiacal types. Everything is done with passionate zeal, which can work violently (the Scorpion) or with high aspiration (the Eagle).

The rulership of Pluto seems the most likely, as Scorpio embodies the urge to throw out obstructions to make way for new life. This is a constant process of refinement and regeneration.

Scorpio will pour effort into worthwhile causes, using a penetrating mind to analyse problems, though more likely to solve them by intuition rather than reason.

An attribute of Scorpio is personal charisma and magnetism. Another is a tendency to be secretive about plans and also to be a good keeper of the secrets of other people. Capable of making sudden changes in life style in response to inner urges, Scorpio surprises others who will not have had any warning of these drastic actions.

SAGITTARIUS (The Archer)

Although this is a Fire sign, Sagittarius is more adaptable than Aries or Leo. Sagittarius is ruled by Jupiter, the planet which signifies expansion, growth and maturity, so the fiery side of Sagittarius is not so apparent.

Still energetic and enthusiastic, but also tolerant and happy-go-lucky in attitude, Sagittarius takes a broad view and does not like to be bothered with details. A lot of interests are enjoyed — many of them superficial — but Sagittarius has a good brain and is capable of deep study.

Sagittarius reacts well to a challenge and the greatest enemy is boredom. Sagittarius is a philosopher who realises the value of detachment from worldly cares and tends to be the perennial optimist.

The Sagittarian's great need is for freedom, both of mind and body; freedom to explore both physically and spiritually. Sagittarius is often a dedicated sportsperson — active, not passive — and hates to feel fenced in.

Like Leo, Sagittarius is capable of planning large projects, but a lack of application to details often means that projects do not get beyond the planning stage. Nevertheless, if the mind can be sufficiently disciplined to tackle one thing at a time, Sagittarius has a great deal of intuitive wisdom to offer.

CAPRICORN (The Goat)

This is the last Earth sign, signifying practicality and resolution. In addition it is ruled by Saturn, the planet of discipline and responsibility. In Capricorn, all this is combined with initiative, so there is a strong ambitious drive to succeed by hard work and perseverance.

Capricorn shows practicality and responsibility at an early age, many children with a Capricorn 'influence' getting on better with older people than with their peers and having 'old heads on young shoulders'.

Capricorn has great patience and is content to take one step at a time. Time is an important consideration — Capricorn never hurries, but seems to have an inbuilt sense of timing and everything is accomplished 'in its own good time'.

Although Capricorn does not represent mental agility, it does signify late development and benefits from further education. The quality which beats all competitors is formidable perseverance. Capricorn wins the race in true 'Tortoise and the Hare' fashion.

Capricornians are good at constructing detailed plans and do not change their minds easily. Capricorn needs security and often looks for it in a stable, lucrative position in the business world. They do not seek the limelight, however, but enjoy the power which a 'top job' can bring. A dry sense of humour is an attribute of Capricorn.

AQUARIUS (The Waterbearer)

Despite its title, this is not a Water sign. It is the third Air sign, signifying the qualities of intellect and communication. It is ruled by Uranus, the planet associated with change, freedom and revolution.

Freedom is as important to Aquarius as to Sagittarius, but Aquarius is more intense about it, guarding freedom jealously and prepared to fight for it, if necessary. Hence, we have the revolutionary attitude. But this is combined with great humanitarian feelings, so that Aquarius is often found fighting for other people's rights.

There is a tendency to be cautious, so revolutionary ideas are often expressed in words, but are not always translated into action.

Usually Aquarius is self-sufficient and self-assured, original, inventive and unconventional, with the courage of conviction. Once Aquarius is sure the ideas are right, it does not matter if he or she is the only one who holds them. This may well happen, for Aquarius is often a pioneer in the field of ideas, but can become utterly eccentric or perhaps a self-opinionated rebel.

On the surface, Aquarius is friendly and enjoys socialising and joining organisations, often those with humanitarian aims. However, Aquarius is not easy to know intimately and can appear rather cold-natured.

PISCES (The Fishes)

The last sign in the zodiac is a Water sign, ruled by Neptune. This planet is associated with intuition and imagination and it combines with the emotional and intuitive qualities of Water to produce a kind of soup through which the Fishes have to swim!

Pisces is full of emotion and imprecise feelings and may therefore appear to live in a perpetual dream-world. The intuition can however be used constructively. Pisces is compassionate, being sympathetic to other people's troubles and always willing to help. Kindness, gentleness and optimism are all attributes of Pisces.

Pisces leads a rich and full inner life, sometimes channelling intuition and feeling for rhythm into poetry or music.

There is a great necessity to escape from all worldly problems, which encourages the tendency to day-dream. A result of this is to make Pisceans adaptable and accommodating to other people, so that they appear to have no opinions of their own.

Pisces has great sensitivity and can become subject to nebulous fears and apprehensions. Often these are only the product of an over-anxious, over-active imagination. Pisces also has a mediumistic type of inner sensitivity.

You will now have an idea of the basic personalities expressed by the sun's position at birth in each of the twelve signs of the zodiac. But the moon sign is in many ways, the most important for our purpose. This is because the moon represents the part of personality which tends to be suppressed as we grow up, for the moon represents the emotions, the unconscious, the instinctive reactions.

As the moon moves quickly, through every sign of the zodiac every month, you can only discover your moon sign by having a birth chart computed (see chapter 3 and page 159). However, if you read through the description of the zodiacal signs again, you may be able to guess the position of your moon, because one description may fit you particularly well in respect of your emotional nature, and especially to your feelings as a child.

Young children express their feelings freely. They leave adults in no doubt as to whether they are happy or sad, contented or angry. As we grow up, we learn to conceal these raw emotions and only rarely become aware of how we are really feeling inside. Psychologists commonly find that depression often masks real anger and it is only when the anger is expressed that the depressed patient begins to recover.

Young children often make decisions *for life* before the age of six on the basis of the circumstances in which they find themselves. Some of these decisions will stand them in good stead for the rest of their lives, while others may no longer apply as circumstances change or as the person grows up. They may nevertheless continue to carry the outdated decision, like excess baggage, for the rest of their lives, little realising how much it is inhibiting their progress.

We can imagine a child who is left parentless at an early age, coming to the conclusion that he or she must look after him- or herself, a decision which may be lived with happily into adult life (though it could make the individual very selfish). But we can also think of a child who is born into a large, noisy, extrovert family, who may find that an easy way to get mother's attention is to play 'poor little me', the quiet child who sits in the corner and sulks, or weeps easily.

If this person goes through life believing that the way to get what he or she wants from the world is to project themselves in this fashion, it is obvious that they are inhibiting themselves and destroying all possibility of achieving their aims. Yet it is amazing how many people fail to realise that an attitude which stood them in good stead as a child is no longer relevant to adult life.

Another reason why children take attitudes which then become habitual is to please the parent. This is a common and natural thing to happen since most of us wish to live peacefully with those on whom, as children, we depend for comfort, sustenance and love. But what a parent required of us as a child, for instance, to let them make all our decisions for us, will not be applicable as we become adult. Many parents themselves do not realise this and may continue to try to make decisions for an adult son or daughter still living at home. In these circumstances, it takes courage for the young adult to insist on taking responsibility for their own life. Sometimes it is not lack of courage, but simply lack of understanding of the situation which prevents them from doing so. They have become so conditioned to believing that they are not capable of taking decisions for themselves that they continue to believe it, sometimes for the whole of their lives, so that they tend to find very decisive life-partners and to depend on them as they did upon the parents.

In the next chapter some ways will be considered in which the different moon signs may give clues to the inhibiting factors which may be at work in the birthchart.

I have not gone into great detail in describing the various zodiacal types, as much more will become apparent about each as their psychological weaknesses, their health and their needs, are considered.

In the next chapter, consideration is given to how you can become your own worst enemy, but first a reminder that none of us is representative of only *one* zodiacal sign. It is likely that the sun and moon are positioned in different signs at birth and when the positions of the planets are considered as well, you will see that most of the signs are likely to play a part in your own psychological make-up.

The zodiac in its entirety represents the complete person, whether or not a particular sign may be emphasised by having a planet in it, so that the individual is equipped with all that is needed to fulfil life's potential.

No birthchart is a 'bad' chart. All are bursting with potential and express the many sidedness of human nature, so that, if one door closes, there are many more just waiting to be opened.

It would be quite wrong to give the impression that life becomes easy and delightful immediately self-awareness is achieved. Life is hard for many people and there may be little that can be done to ease that hardship. But humankind has often shown its best qualities at times of extreme hardship for the human spirit is not easily quenched. It is the little things that get us down; we rise to the grand challenge, but fall prey to minor fears.

The command of the great oracle at Delphi was 'Man, know thyself', but even today few of us are aware of the many facets of our personalities that are suppressed — and in how many ways. Working at the task of becoming what we truly are, we will be able to break free from the mould of past conditioning, develop and strengthen our will-power, use our aggressive drive constructively so that we may achieve, discover our intuitive and creative abilities and, above all, feel a sense of personal freedom.

Do not expect this to happen quickly in a great blaze of sudden insight. It is such an experience for a minority of people, but for most the goal is achieved by small steps forward with the occasional set back. It is not easy to break patterns which have been self-imposed over many years, but every small triumph reinforces new insights, until, at last, it becomes habitual to take a new-found freedom for granted.

2
PROGRAMMED FOR FAILURE?

Are you satisfied with your life? If not, which facets of it cause you most problems?

If you find these questions difficult to answer, take time before you read further to do the following exercise.

Close your eyes and visualise the rest of your life as you expect it to be. What about your career, your relationships, your health, your personal aims and achievements? Think about each of these for a few minutes. Now imagine that your life is drawing to its earthly end. Look back over the situations you have visualised and be aware of your feelings. Has it been a good life? A life worth living? Have you achieved many of the goals that you set yourself? What about the one which mattered most to you? Have your hopes been fulfilled?

If the answers to most of these questions are negative, I have good news for you. You can change that ending. But I also have a warning — *only you* can do it. You can learn from other people and from books. You can even go to classes which will help you to gain insights and which will teach you that you are not alone in your quest for the power to take charge of your own life. But in the final analysis no-one else can do it for you.

Distrust anyone who tells you (or implies) otherwise. There is no shortage of 'Agony Aunts', counsellors of various types, astrologers, clairvoyants — the list is endless — who may be able to help you by discussion, or by giving an outsider's summary of a situation, but decisions must be yours, just as any action can only be taken by you. All good counsellors are aware of this and will not seek to take away your own autonomy by telling you what to do.

But where do you start? First of all, you must define the problem. What has been holding you back? Consider a few possibilities: a natural timidity, a feeling of responsibility for someone else, lack of self-confidence, a quick temper, a dread of unpleasantness, undue sensitivity to criticism, lack of willpower or energy, ill-health, feelings of inferiority.

Another piece of good news — you are not unique. Everyone of us has some psychological hang-ups. I have only mentioned a few causes of problems and already you may have identified several as being appropriate to you.

Almost any childhood pattern has within it the seeds of potential failure, or success, in later life and where difficult conditions are reinforced by inherent tendencies, inhibitions and complexes may become strong. A child who tends to be fearful by nature may be born to overprotective parents who can undermine the child's self-confidence still further. An adventurous child born to the same parents will naturally benefit since their nurturing will help to balance his or her natural bent.

In searching for self-development, what Jung called 'individuation', we need to affirm that we have as much right to a fulfilled life as any other person. As far as is known there may be only one lifetime and we should not feel that we have to sacrifice that life to any cause or any other person unless that is what we really wish to do. There are cases where a sacrificial life can be self-fulfilling, but there are many more where one person is sacrificed to another's selfishness.

Let me teach you the first rule of individuation. No-one can force you to do anything without your consent. If you are subordinating your life to someone else, that is *your* decision. If someone tries to hurt you or put you down, it is up to you whether or not they succeed. If you refuse to feel hurt or put down they will fail in their object and soon stop trying. It is not easy to cultivate this detached attitude with someone you love, but it can be done and need not harm the love between you. It may strengthen it, as the other person comes to accept you as someone who has equal rights with them to live the life you want.

It should be easier to be detached with people who do not matter to us emotionally, yet many of us allow acquaintances to put us down. It could be rather devastating to have someone tell you that you are not very bright, for instance, but how satisfying to reply 'that's just your opinion' with the implication that you have no respect for their opinion — and it's even better to feel it!

As you begin the process of changing the attitudes which have held you back, you will find how true it is that people accept us at our own valuation. When you show that you put a high value on yourself and your opinions you will find that others look at you with new eyes.

I have a friend who is a successful female executive in the male world of heavy transport. She finds in her travels and attendances at business conferences that she gets better treatment than her position entitles her to, because she acts as though it was her right and her expectation. She does not need to be aggressive, ultra-feminine or haughty. She feels 'special' so she is accepted as 'special'. We should all feel like this, for each of us is unique.

None of the foregoing implies that we should not have close relationships with other people. In fact they are necessary to our survival. Babies who are not loved become ill and may even die. In the same way, everyone feels the need to be loved by some people, appreciated by others and recognised as a person by all those with whom they come into contact. The essence of loneliness has been summed up in the words, 'If no-one recognises my existence, I feel that I do not exist.'

What we need for ourselves we cannot deny to others. We all need good feelings which we get from being recognised by others. If you say 'Good morning' to your colleague, you have recognised that he is there. If he does not respond you may feel hurt or, 'put down' because he has not similarly recognised you. You should be able to shrug it off and think, probably correctly, 'Old Fred's still half-asleep' and not bother with him until later in the day. But even a self-sufficient person would begin to feel concerned with no recognition from anyone. This is why people who are suffering from depression are so often told to go and join a club. If they are seeing no-one they will not get the appreciative recognition which is necessary for survival.

We should also be aware that other people sometimes try to put us down because they are not getting any 'stroking' themselves, to use a psychological term, and making us feel bad makes them feel better. In effect they are giving themselves a 'negative stroke' which is better than no 'stroke' at all. If someone perpetually does this to you, it will help you not to feel 'put down' if you see this person as someone to be pitied, someone who is feeling unloved. If you can give them the love, or at least the appreciation, which they are missing, you may be pleasantly surprised to see them blossom into likeable people.

The astrological signs which are given prominence in the birthchart, can indicate clearly where psychological difficulties are likely to be and will show basic needs. The moon sign is often the one which is most indicative, but the sun sign and the Ascending sign can also give valuable clues. In considering each of them again, I shall be emphasising the negative aspects of the

31

personality, but remember that each sign also has its strengths. Read through them all, as you may have an important planet in one which will make it particularly applicable.

THE FIRE SIGNS

It is the nature of the Fire signs to be outgoing, active and energetic, but this natural property may be inhibited by parental restrictions, or it may be overemphasised. In the latter case, a person may suffer from taking on more work or responsibilities than they can reasonably be expected to do. This may result in health difficulties or in feelings of resentment. People who complain that they are always left to do everything never see that the fault is their own. I repeat that no-one can make you do anything unless you let them.

But more often, the Fire type who has programmed him or herself for failure is still inhibited by feelings that a natural enthusiasm should be curbed. I have an Arien friend who has a great deal of wisdom and knowledge which people recognise as valuable as soon as she starts to speak. The difficulty is to get her to start. I told her one day that she should be speaking from a platform. She did not say that she was not qualified to do so, nor that she was nervous, but simply, 'Oh, I couldn't put myself forward in that way.'

It would appear that her natural exuberance had been put down as self-aggrandisement when she was younger and she had taken that unlovely picture of herself to heart.

I told her what every lecturer knows. 'The audience is not interested in you, but only in what you have to give them. If you have something to say, speak up. The speech is more important than the speaker.'

This was quite a new idea to her. I saw that she had been conditioned to believe that everyone who had chosen to do something which put them in front of the public 'thought themselves somebody' and that, even if they did not perform in a 'showing-off' way, they had the sort of confidence in themselves which made them seem superior to her. She had a feeling of inferiority in their presence which made her feel 'put down' and which she resented. She projected this feeling of resentment onto them and had convinced herself that they were unlikeable people, not the sort of person she would wish to emulate. This was a way of giving herself a negative stroke, since she can now consider herself superior to them.

This is quite a common way for **Aries** to inhibit personal capabilities, since the natural urge is for leadership and pioneering. Aries' ruling planet, Mars, relates in physical terms to the adrenal system and almost all performers will tell you that they need that shot of adrenalin, often experienced as fear, in order to give a good performance. Soldiers under fire know that bravery is not the lack of fear, and the Arien type has the sort of courage which shows up in dangerous situations.

The world needs the Arien's courage and leadership and it is a great pity that it should so often be denied to us by Ariens themselves who, through parental training or feelings of inadequacy, inhibit the natural expression of their own personalities.

The Arien is also capable of considerable self-sacrifice. If this is made willingly, with a full appreciation of all that it entails, it can be life-enhancing. I have known of at least one partnership where the Arien partner recognised before marriage that her proposed husband had important work to do and not too much time in which to accomplish it. Only her devotion enabled him to carry it through. She might have been brilliant in her own sphere, but voluntarily chose to give up all thought of this. Her husband fully appreciated what she had done and she felt completely rewarded and fulfilled.

On the other side of the coin, I remember a sad German woman who had been forced by a dominating father to devote her life to looking after her parents. He had insisted on her becoming a school teacher, a career which she disliked and for which she had no vocation. When I met her, both parents were dead, but she felt that it was much too late to make a new life for herself. I shall never forget what she said to me. 'I feel that I have nothing and I am nothing.' She was helped by friends who lived near her to make a new beginning, but what a waste of fifty years.

I am quite sure that most parents would never knowingly do this to their children, nor husbands to their wives, but so many do not realise it. When the victim begins to take responsibility for his or her own life and refuses to allow anyone to dictate how they should live, a new relationship develops (not, of course, without initial difficulties) and often results in both parties taking a more healthy attitude to each other. In some cases, it results in the end of a partnership or friendship, but this is usually a belated recognition of the true state of affairs.

The Arien is naturally aggressive. This is a neutral trait, in exactly the same way as are patience, adaptability, or any other characteristic you care to name. That is to say that it is available for use in either a positive or negative manner, but is not in itself either good or bad.

Aggression can be used well, to help the achievement of a legitimate aim; it is bad when it is turned against others in a violent manner; it is crippling if it is turned against oneself.

Many psychological difficulties are caused by self-aggression, not the least an active fear of violence because the victim is frightened of their own strong feelings and is determined to suppress them. This may result in the sacrifice of the self to others as we have seen and an apparent willingness to let other people have their own way at all times. This can end in Ariens losing their sense of identity with resulting health difficulties, which will be discussed later. Alternatively, there may be a smouldering resentment for the situation, which could break out into physical violence. The world may see such a person as 'always having a chip on their shoulder'.

If they appreciate the cause of their trouble and learn to use aggression positively, all inhibitions can be overcome. Ways of doing this will be considered in a later chapter.

The next Fire sign, **Leo**, has a need to be creative and to display talents with pride. As a child, the Leo native is likely to be a show-off and to be bossy. Naturally, parents will try to control these traits, but if the child is made to feel that such characteristics are unacceptable and make him unloveable, he may develop into a person who is actually afraid of being capable, lest he should be accused of being dominating or domineering.

This is all the more likely if 'he' is actually 'she', since females are still seen as being 'aggressive', whereas their male counterparts would be described as 'go-getters'.

The fact that Leo types have a great deal of dignity enables them to conceal their feelings well, but this means that inhibitions can be built up because they do not express their anger or the hurt which they feel. Leo's deep-rooted urge to put a good face on things may result in a familiar pattern, with which they feel safe, of acceptance of an inferior position, or of domination by someone else, which is in complete contrast to their natural bent and denies them the opportunity to be the leader, for which they are so well fitted.

Sagittarians in their pursuit of freedom sometimes have a dread of responsibility, since they feel that this may limit them. These are the people who are quite capable of throwing a spanner in the works and defeating their own ends quite unconsciously. They may be in line for a promotion which the real self desires, but the part of them which feels threatened by the resultant discipline may suddenly decide to throw up their job altogether and look for something less demanding, or they may miss an important interview by being late or feeling ill.

Their love of variety can also inhibit them from achieving their aims because they find it difficult to harness their willpower. Their energy tends to lack direction. They are explorers, but it sometimes seems that they are always looking, but not finding. There is a psychological reason for this: if they find, they can stop looking, and looking is what they like to do, or have been conditioned to do.

One particular psychological therapy refers to 'life scripts'. People allocate themselves a part to play, often in early childhood, and tend to play it into adult life until it is outgrown (sometimes this never happens). While they are playing the part, they are stuck with it because they do not see what else they can do. So with the Sagittarian, who has the part of the explorer, if he or she found what they were seeking what could be done then? They would have 'lost their part' and cease to exist. So people have a vested interest in playing their chosen part whether it be the constant worker, the perpetual invalid, the perennial optimist — everyone who is always in the same category is likely to be locked into a life script. People who have started the real process of inner growth cannot be classified in this way, since the 'real self' has so many facets.

THE EARTH SIGNS

I have said that the Earth signs are all practical and reliable, so you may think that they would have little difficulty in adjusting to life. This is not so because life is full of risks and change and the Earth types tend to resent both. Taureans, Virgoans and Capricornians are the people who are most likely to put up with a difficult situation because they feel safer with the established position, however unpleasant, than to risk breaking away from the familiar pattern.

This is particularly true of the **Taureans** with their need for a firm base. They can show resourcefulness in achieving this, especially in terms of finance and acquiring valuable possessions. They have an unsurpassed appreciation of value in all tangible things, but do not bring the same judgement to bear on the quality of their own lives. They can get locked into unsatisfactory relationships or jobs for no better reason than that they offer security. Whether the security is worth having on these terms is something which never seems to occur to them.

The Taurean may find it more difficult than most types to find self-fulfilment, since the process requires them to recognise the possibility of change and also to *want* to change. This is against their nature, but the reward is the greatest that could be hoped for; nothing less than a sense of security which is based on the assurance that they are capable of coping with anything which life may throw at them. This inner security is the ultimate goal of all of us in the search for self-fulfilment.

The **Virgoan** is much more adaptable than the Taurean in many ways, but the Virgoan rigidity shows in the attitude to all that is undertaken. Virgoans set a standard of perfection, thus programming themselves for failure from the very beginning. No wonder that they lack self-confidence, since they have forbidden themselves to succeed at anything! This does not stop them from trying hard, often continuing with an impossible task long after others would have abandoned it, so that they are perpetually frustrated and complain bitterly that nothing they do ever seems to go right.

One of the psychological therapies describes parental injunctions which are known as 'hookers' — because, if you try to obey them, you get 'hooked' into impossible situations. The Virgoan seems to be at the mercy of several of these, which are implicit in their own natures, rather than being the result of parental training, though this may reinforce them. One of these hookers is, 'Be perfect', the hooker being that it is unforgivable to make mistakes. Remember though that one way of learning is by making mistakes. Another one which applies to the

37

Virgoan is, 'Try hard'. Here the hooker is 'Don't succeed, because if you do you can stop trying'. Yet a third is, 'Work hard' and the hooker — 'Don't finish'.

The fact that the Virgoan also tries to apply their own standards to others is something which will be considered when personal relationships are discussed.

The **Capricornian's** rigidity is exercised over feelings. My Capricorn brother-in-law met me at the station in his car on a rainy night and halfway home, about eight miles from the station, the engine spluttered and died. We were in the middle of the country. He walked to the nearest house, phoned the AA and patiently waited until someone arrived, a good while later. The car then started at first try, the wet sparking plugs having dried by then. He drove the rest of the way without a word of complaint. Both myself and my sister are married to Virgoans — we agreed that they would have both expressed themselves forcibly and then blamed themselves all the way home. I am sure my Capricorn brother-in-law felt equally annoyed and frustrated, but he would have felt a lot worse if he had shown his feelings to me.

Capricornians want certitude and constancy in their lives in true Earth native fashion and they welcome control, either having it imposed on them or imposing it on themselves. Some of them glory in their apparent lack of emotion and will convey the message, 'I have had a hard life, but I can take it'. However, bottling up emotions can cause both physical and psychological difficulties. A warning to all parents of a Capricorn child, never tell them to 'keep a stiff upper lip' or that 'big boys don't cry'. You will be reinforcing a pattern which is already strong and may do untold harm. Children who have had a parental injunction, 'Don't show your feelings', end up with the hooker, 'It is wrong to feel emotion'. These are the people who become unaware of their true feelings and may show symptoms of depression when they are really very angry.

THE AIR SIGNS

The signs of the Air triplicity, Gemini, Libra and Aquarius, are all represented by people who are mentally active and can appear emotionally cold, although this is less true of Libra than the others. In a sense, they all wish to distance themselves from other people at a deeper level and tend to keep their contacts with others friendly, but superficial.

The **Geminian**, like the opposite sign, the Sagittarian, has difficulties with exercising willpower, and tends to give up or give in easily. This may be reinforced by childhood patterns or may be because it is simply less trouble, but it does mean that Geminians are easily manipulated by others. They are afraid of emotional involvements because they quickly get nervous and distressed by seeing people in an emotional state whether it be in the form of quarrels, tears or passion. There is a distrust of their own feelings so that they cultivate a detached manner which strikes others as cold.

Depression can result from deep feelings of loneliness and also from allowing others to restrict the natural inclination to follow many pursuits at the same time. Adaptability needs to be expressed and Gemini children who are over-controlled by their parents may become withdrawn, instead of being the lively people that they are by nature.

Self-deception is a danger with these people so that they may be unaware of their true feelings until they have done some work on themselves. The nature of this work will be discussed in a later chapter.

Although **Librans** are the children of Venus and therefore not so distant in manner as Gemini, they also have the instinct to distance themselves from all that is unpleasant. They have a dread of quarrels, sleazy places, or scenes of deprivation. Preferring not to think about such things, they can live an unrealistic life wrapped in their own cocoons and not appreciating that they will never emerge as butterflies if they continue to hide away from life.

Such an attitude makes them vulnerable to all the nasty knocks which life can bring and they will make matters worse by feeling that they are more badly treated than anyone else. People who are sorry for themselves do not get much sympathy and so this attitude can create a vicious circle making Librans feel even more that they are being unjustly treated.

Decisions are difficult at the best of times for the Libran native, they are inclined to accept what life has done *to* them as though they had no say in the matter at all. Their script is 'the victim of circumstances'. With such an attitude, it is not surprising that they frequently blame the other person. It is never their fault.

Aquarians, with a strong desire for freedom, find it difficult to commit themselves to a lasting relationship. Even when they do so, it is common to hear the partner say, 'But I never feel that I really know him'.

We should all have a private life. A great deal of growth goes on within us which is not available to others, even our nearest and dearest, and we should all respect each other's need for this privacy. Not to do so involves us in the devouring type of love which can destroy. But deep relationships are only made if they are to be rooted securely. This is something which Aquarians do not seem to realise. They are so fearful of feeling trapped that they overlook the need to trust other people.

There are two ways in which this situation can become inhibiting. One is becoming suspicious of everyone. The other can be the realisation of the power inherent in denying closeness to others. This is a devastating thing to do to those in close relationship and may lead to loneliness and despair as the others gradually break free from such an inhibiting situation.

All the Air signs are afraid of getting involved with life and tend to live it on the surface. This leaves them with no resources to cope with real crises, so that they then choose psychological or physical illness to enable them to retreat from these situations.

THE WATER SIGNS

The Water signs, being emotional and intuitive, are full of feeling for other people and find difficulty in coping on their own. While it is good to feel and to express emotions, they should not rule us, for we are not just our emotions.

The great psychotherapist, Dr Roberto Assagioli, gave his students an exercise to emphasise this point which consisted of them recognising and repeating that:

I have a body, but *I* am not my body.
I have a mind, but *I* am not my mind.
I have feelings, but *I* am not my feelings,

and so on. This is something which we all need to recognise.

The **Cancerian**, being a home lover, likes the safety of the familiar and tends to dwell in the past, which is known, rather than the unknown future. They can react negatively to challenges, feeling, 'I am too weak for this. I want to feel safe'.

The mother is likely to be the dominant parent for the Cancerian child, so the mother's attitude is likely to influence the whole life. If she encourages the child to tackle difficulties, the Cancerian will be more positive, though still looking for mother's approval. If she is overprotective, the child's basic life pattern is reinforced and he or she may become fearful of anything new. In both cases, adult Cancerians are likely to be dependent on the goodwill of others. If it is not forthcoming, they will feel unloved or unappreciated and resentful.

They need to feel that they belong to a family and feel threatened if the family gradually disintegrates. *Self*-fulfilment is, therefore, a difficult task, but a most rewarding one for the Cancerian.

Unless they are well aware of their limitations and know how to overcome them, **Scorpio** natives are at the mercy of their own intensity. They become passionately committed to whatever they undertake, but feel that 'they' will stop them from doing it, or will not approve. This accounts for their secrecy which can amount to deception. Sometimes they let 'what other people will think' stop them from taking actions which they feel instinctively are right for them, but they will then be resentful or vengeful and blame the other person.

A Scorpio man, the father of a schoolfriend of mine, was the manager of a shoe shop. After he formed a liaison with one of his employees, he and his heartbroken wife eventually separated. Divorce was very difficult in those days and it is unlikely that she would have taken the necessary steps in any case. His excuse for his conduct was that his wife had never backed him up in his desire to open a shop of his own. He had always seemed to me a very dominating person. In fact, as a child, I was rather afraid of him, yet it appears that he felt the need for his wife's full approval though she was such an acquiescent person that he would have had no difficulty in going ahead with his project.

The Scorpion's intensity can be frightening in a quarrel. They will not leave the subject of it alone, but continue to let their feelings carry them along until they can erupt in a destructive or jealous rage. They will then feel equally remorseful, to the extent that they may become quite devastated by it.

On the other hand, an appreciation of how deeply they feel anger can cause them to bottle up emotions until something just has to give and again there may be acute depression, which is really hiding anger. The natural propensity for secrecy seems to inhibit the Scorpio native from expressing annoyance when it first occurs and when it could be dealt with at a less intense level of feeling.

The **Piscean** has been described as a 'poor fish' and it is quite true that they do not have the stomach for a fight if they can avoid it. If it is a case of 'fight or flight' they are always more likely to choose flight. They like to live in an ideal dreamworld and it is 'other people' who prevent them, just as it is 'they' who cause all their troubles, since *they* are not in the business of causing trouble. In fact, their motto could be, 'Anything for a quiet life'. This puts them at the mercy of other people from whom they accept the injunction, 'Please me', with the hooker attached, 'Don't please yourself'. Their amazing receptivity makes them immediately aware of what others require of them and they will react at once. No wonder that they, who most desire to stay out of trouble, are the ones who so often find it.

The instinct for escape is thus reinforced and can take the form of drink, drugs, or psychotic conditions.

Another escape can be found in deception or self-deception. I have a Piscean sun sign and I had a strong, 'Be a *good* girl' message from my mother and my grandmother. The result was that I went to a great deal of trouble, not to say low cunning, to conceal my misdemeanours from them. My excuse was that they would have been shocked, so it was kinder to them not to let them know — a good illustration of both deception and self-deception!

This chapter has deliberately emphasised the worst character-istics of each of the signs. Many people will not experience anything like the strength of the inhibitions I have been describ-ing and many more will have weakness in one zodiacal sign balanced by the strength in another. For instance, a Geminian sun sign exhibiting weakness of willpower may be more than compensated by Mars in Capricorn, say, which has the will to succeed and the perseverance to back it.

The birth chart shows the psychological tendencies which we bring into life with us, but these will be modified, perhaps strengthened, by parental attitudes and our own life experiences, so do not be downcast by the descriptions in this chapter.

On the other hand, do not think that you are completely free from hang-ups just because you do not recognise the ones I have described. This is how I felt when I first started investigating psychology and psychotherapy, but I soon discovered my mis-take.

One day I realised that I instinctively smiled at anyone who met my eye, whether I felt like smiling or not. In true Piscean fashion I was saying, 'I'm friendly. Like me, I won't hurt you. Please don't hurt me.' I knew that I had made a big step forward when I could smile or not, just as I felt. It was going a little way towards being truly myself.

Self-awareness and then the courage to be that self becomes self-fulfilment.

3
SELF-PROJECTION AND THE BIRTH CHART

So that we can form a more complete idea of the picture of individual personality that the birth chart presents to us, we will consider in this chapter two more important ingredients. First, the Ascendant, or Rising Sign, and then the astrological houses.

From your birth chart you will be able to see that there is a horizontal axis which is marked with an arrow on the left-hand side. This is often labelled 'Asc' or 'Ascendant'. The sign of the zodiac in which this is positioned is called the Rising Sign, and this is an important indicator of the type of personality that we like to present or project to the world.

The position of the Ascendant indicates the sign of the zodiac that was 'rising' over the eastern horizon at the time of your birth.

The interpretation of the Ascendant is 'the face we show to the world'.

Many acquaintances would not recognise us by sun sign traits which are often revealed only to those who know us well, nor by our moon sign since we do not usually register much emotion with colleagues at work, our boss or the people we meet casually.

Instead, we tend to project ourselves in the way in which we want them to see us and often that is the way in which we see ourselves. We all like to think that we are whatever seems most desirable to us, hearty, reserved, charming, outspoken, diplomatic and so on. Because we value these traits and try to project them, they become a valid part of the personality. We are not showing a false face to the world, but rather portraying the person we would like to be.

As with the sun signs, the Ascendant can indicate both strengths and weaknesses, so it is as well to know what you may unwittingly reveal to others.

Aries Rising. If the Ascendant is in Aries, you may want to project yourself as enthusiastic, dynamic, quick-thinking, etc., but overemphasis of these characteristics may make you appear overbearing, quick-tempered and restless.

Taurus Rising. Similarly, the Taurean type who values solid worth and practicality may come over to other people as a bore without a glimmer of originality.

Gemini Rising. The Gemini Ascendant portrays the 'bright-eyed and bushytailed' extrovert, who can easily get the reputation of being superficial.

Cancer Rising. Cancerian mother or father figures show sympathy and kindness, but this can easily become unwanted interference in other people's lives.

Leo Rising. Everyone recognises the man or woman with a Leo Ascendant — the hearty handshake, the bright smile, the warmth of personality, but, oh dear, it is overwhelming and can easily seem bogus.

Virgo Rising. The Virgoan's capability is self-evident, but so is the propensity to fuss with every little detail and to insist that everything is done their way and to their exacting standards.

Libra Rising. The charm of Libra makes an immediate impact, but disillusion can soon set in when their indolence and indecisiveness are revealed.

Scorpio Rising. Here is the Scorpio personality, magnetic, flatteringly interested in you, but a bit frightening in their intensity and with a biting tongue.

Sagittarius Rising. Sagittarian tolerant good humour is attractive, but there is a lack of real concern for others, which soon becomes apparent.

Capricorn Rising. Although those with a Capricorn Ascendant appear to be patient, hardworking people, the really ambitious ones can be quite ruthless in their way up the ladder of success.

Aquarius Rising. You will meet Aquarians in every club or society. They are so supportive in a group and everyone likes them. Perhaps this is the best Ascendant to have, since the Aquarian tendency to shrink from close relationships does not matter with superficial acquaintances. The Aquarian attitude to more permanent relationships will be considered in the next chapter.

Pisces Rising. People with Piscean Ascendants are instantly likeable, being warm, friendly and anxious to please, but they can get tedious when you find that they agree with you all the time.

We now have the three basic ingredients of a psychological make-up; the sun representing the basic personality, the moon showing the emotional responses and personality, and the Ascendant, the projected personality. The mixture of these three creates the fascinating, complex human being.

THE HOUSES

Each of the twelve houses represents a different area of life, in which the planetary energies may act. There are several systems of dividing the birth chart into houses. Because there is no agreement among astrologers on the best system to use, I do not consider that the meanings of the houses are precise, they tend to overlap, but I will give them here as they are usually defined.

The houses are numbered from the Ascendant in an anticlockwise direction, so that the house immediately below the Ascendant is house number one.

The first house is concerned with the personality and any planet in this house is emphasised or 'strong'. Like the Ascendant, it also represents the person as seen by others.

The second house refers to possessions, finance and all that is needed to sustain life in a material sense.

The third house refers to communications and education, but also to near relatives and neighbours.

The fourth house is known as the house of the home. If the sun is in this house you need to have a secure base and are likely to be a home maker.

The fifth house relates to creativity, sport and children.

The sixth house is the house of work and health.

The seventh house is the realm of partnerships, marriage and relationships.

The eighth house refers to matters of life and death. It has connotations with hidden (occult) matters.

The ninth house is associated with further education, long journeys and matters connected with foreign people and places.

The tenth house relates to career, social status and public life.

The eleventh house refers to groups and societies and to wider issues affecting many people.

The twelfth house indicates matters of privacy and suggests seclusion or protected environments such as hospitals, schools, prisons, or monasteries. A planet here suggests that privacy is needed in some area of life.

The house indications can be summed up by saying that planets positioned in the bottom half of the chart (north) refer to the private life and planets in the top half (south) refer to public life. Planets on the left (east) refer solely to the person who is represented by the birth chart, while planets on the right (west) refer to relationships and contacts with others.

An astrologer who was interpreting a birth chart would also look at the contact which each planet makes to each of the others and would obtain a lot of information, some of which would be contradictory. It is part of the astrologer's art to decide which of the many facets of character revealed by the chart are dominant and of significance.

In some cases, the astrologer may decide that two traits are equally important and that the person should make time for both of them. For instance, a chart may show that drive and energy is being put into a career, while a loving relationship at home is just as important to the career man or woman. If this is so, a balance needs to be struck between the time and attention given to each.

You will see that astrology can be complicated, but if it appeals to you and you decide to study it, you will find it a fascinating subject, which will give valuable insights into the characters of other people.

4
RELATIONSHIPS, VENUS AND MARS

Every person is a complex being and this complexity is highlighted by the many paradoxes of human nature.

In order to achieve self-fulfilment we need to recognise that each of us is unique and in a fundamental way we are all alone. This implies detachment from our fellow beings and it is true that we need to establish and assert our absolute sovereignty over our own lives. No other individual should be given the power to dictate to us — and if they *have* that power, it is because we have given it to them. We have surrendered our sovereignty and we must regain it, if we are ever to achieve full potential.

At the same time, we need other people; as comrades, as colleagues, as loved ones. If we do not establish such relationships we shall fail to satisfy some of our essential requirements for complete fulfilment.

This particular paradox is reconciled by making contracts, either implicitly or actually. An employer is given certain rights by his employee in return for wages and conditions to which both agree. Should the contract prove unsatisfactory to either party, it can be terminated. We make an implied contract with our children when we decide to have them, that we will look after them until they are adult and we imply certain contracts in our other relationships also.

The danger with contracts, as any lawyer will tell you, arises when they do not clearly specify the intentions of each party. If a contract is only implicit it is likely that both parties to it may take certain things for granted which are not intended by the other.

Too often the existence of love, whether it be between marriage partners, friends or relations is taken by one of the parties to mean that the other is prepared to do anything for them or even that the other person *should* do what they want. This is particularly true of the husband–wife and parent–child relationship, and if it is accepted by the other party without protest, they have already abdicated their right to their own life. No-one has the right to run someone else's life as well as their own. What we want for ourselves, we must be prepared to grant to others.

The Gestalt therapists have a 'prayer' which is worth quoting here:

'I do my thing and you do your thing. I am not in this world to live up to your expectations. And you are not in this world to live up to mine. You are you and I am I, And if, by chance, we find each other, it's beautiful, If not, it can't be helped.'

This is a healthy attitude and one which we should all feel. Love and goodwill may lead us to make concessions to others and often we will do so because we want to, but it is not a sign of love to give other people the right to rule our lives — it is a sign of weakness. We are relying on them in situations where we should be self-reliant.

In our day-to-day relationships we want to get on well with other people, so that life is pleasant for us. In our closer relationships we need to give and receive love.

Since the birth chart can show our psychological nature so clearly, comparison of two people's charts can show not only whether they are basically compatible but also where their relationship will be strong and where difficulties are likely to be encountered. Astrologers call such a comparison 'synastry' (syn = together, astra = a star). This is a valuable tool to supply information to those wishing to enter into a partnership, business, marriage, or whatever, and it is being used increasingly as people become aware of the technique.

You cannot decide whether two people are compatible just from knowing their sun signs. Traditionally, all the Fire and Air signs are compatible with each other, and so are the Air and Water signs. But suppose you have a Gemini (Air) sun, and your partner has a Scorpio (Water) sun. While you may think this makes you incompatible, the astrologer may see that you have a Scorpio moon and your partner has a Gemini Ascendant. These would be strong links and denote a lasting partnership. Since the emotions are emphasised in a loving relationship, marriage partners who have the same moon sign will express their feelings in the same way and are likely to make a successful marriage.

The Ascendant, sun and moon positions in the birth chart indicate the psychological nature, in terms of basic personality, emotions, and projected personality. While these remain the strongest indications in the chart, the positions of each of the other planets refer to facets of our characters and it is the planet Venus which shows how we make and maintain personal relationships.

51

One of the joys of astrology is that it teaches us to be more tolerant and to appreciate the difficulties of other people. The emotional and warmhearted employee may find it extremely difficult to relate to a cold and stern Virgoan or Capricornian boss. How helpful it can be to realise that he or she may actually be fearful — the Virgoan of failure, the Capricornian of his or her own emotional nature; sympathetic understanding can make all the difference to a relationship of this kind.

The same applies to closer relationships. People who are afraid of the criticism of others will suspect implied criticism when it is not present. If the partner is aware of this, reassurance that no criticism is intended helps a great deal and it also makes the other person aware of what they are doing *to themselves*. "I feel guilty about leaving you to do the washing up", said by a Piscean wife, who had been busy doing another vital task, received the matter-of-fact reply, "Well, I can't help you feeling guilty if you want to, but *I* am not responsible for your feelings."

When you are reading through the descriptions of Venus in the different signs remember that this planet also has to do with values. What you value in life is indicated by the sign in which Venus appears, as well as your attitude to relationships.

I will now explain how the effect of this planet is interpreted when positioned in each of the zodiacal signs. Remember, when you are considering an appropriate interpretation, that the sun sign (and especially the moon sign, since it deals with the emotions) will also be relevant. This means that you can get some insight, not only about your own attitude to relationships, but also the attitudes of your colleagues and companions.

VENUS IN ARIES

If Venus is in Aries in your birth chart, you are likely to make friendships quickly and easily. You will probably be ardent and demonstrative in love. Difficulties can arise if you have the Arien tendency to be selfish, although this will be less likely if your sun and moon are in different signs. It is likely that you will be an idealist and you may be forever seeking the perfect partner. If your attitude is too unrealistic you are likely to feel 'let down' by partners and friends because they cannot measure up to the standards you have tried to force on them.

If you find it difficult to keep lovers or friends, consider whether break-ups have been due to this attitude on your part. If so, you need to recognise that you are not letting other people be themselves. Genuine affection is felt for people as they really are, 'warts and all'. However, it is also realistic to accept that no-one wants to be on friendly terms with everyone. As the Gestalt prayer said, 'If we find each other, it's beautiful — If not, it can't be helped.' Ariens are easily 'rubbed up the wrong way' and tend to be abrasive themselves when offended. Remember, no-one can make you feel like this, unless you let them.

VENUS IN TAURUS

Whether you have a Taurean sun sign or Venus in Taurus, you are likely to be strongly Taurean, since this is the sign which Venus rules. These people make reliable friends and loving partners. Being natives of Venus they enjoy all beautiful things so they are usually deeply sensual. They tend to be possessive and easily aroused to jealousy which can destroy both close relationships and the ordinary day-to-day ones. Some of them lack generosity, not only with possessions but also in spirit, so that they may become jealous if someone else has some good luck. They are quick to imagine that others are being better treated than themselves. In work conditions, if there is a promotion in the offing, they may resent the colleague who gets it, even though they were obviously the best person for the job.

In emotional relationships, the Taurean needs to learn to 'hold close with open hands', which is the only way we can keep anyone's affection, since we are all free human beings if we choose to take that freedom. Jealousy and possessiveness have destroyed so many relationships which might otherwise have been rewarding, since the other party just will not tolerate such attitudes — and rightly so. None of us belongs to anyone else. We may enter into a contract with another in which we implicitly or actually agree to 'love, honour and cherish' them, but that does not mean that we have agreed to surrender our own autonomy over our lives.

Since the Taurean will be as anxious to give love as to receive it, he or she may easily become the victim of their partner's possessiveness (especially if the partner also has Taurus or Scorpio prominent in the chart). If these difficulties are recognised and avoided, Taurean relationships are likely to be close and enduring.

VENUS IN GEMINI

If Venus is in Gemini, it is probable that few relationships will be deep and lasting. As always, this is likely to be balanced if the moon is in an emotional sign. The Geminian tends to treat all relationships coolly and light heartedly. They look for people with whom they have mental interests in common.

Although capable of affection, they may be inconsistent and will enjoy many flirtations.

Colleagues and friends are likely to be those who are mentally stimulating to them and closer relationships must also be satisfactory on this level.

The Geminian will not tolerate possessiveness and may mistake normal acts of caring for it. This can be most hurtful to others and may eventually drive them away.

The wife of such a person said to him one night as he went out, "Take care." It was said almost casually, but he responded angrily, "Oh, stop fussing round me." The friend who was with him remarked gently, "I just heard your wife tell you that she loves you."

54

Many people (not only Geminians) mistake reminders, which may save them much trouble, for undue criticism, instead of recognising the caring which has prompted them. This is likely to have started in childhood when a mother will continually remind a young child to put a coat on before going out, or to be careful crossing the road. At an early age, the child may resent this, not recognising the maternal love which prompts it, but just feeling that 'mother is always on at me'. We should update this childish resentment as we become mature and recognise that people who do not care for us do not bother to caution us.

VENUS IN CANCER

Of course, it can be overdone and become 'smother love' and the person most likely to do it is the one who has moon or Venus in Cancer. He or she will be caring and protective and the partner will probably enjoy the feeling of being cherished. When carried to the extreme, however, such an attitude can become claustrophobic and clinging. Cancerians often find it difficult to let their children go from the nest, with the result that the more confident ones often leave home earlier than they would otherwise have done.

The Cancerian also needs to feel loved and protected. Their emotions run high and they tend to worry about relations and relationships. This makes it easy for them to feel 'put down' even when there is no cause. They are so concerned about other people that they feel the others should be concerned about them in return and casualness or neglect on the part of a near relation will wound them deeply.

In more casual relationships their warmheartedness and sympathy often result in them taking on the troubles of other people. They will never lack friends because of their helpfulness, but they will become upset if they find that other people are not so sympathetic when they are in need of help.

The process of self-fulfilment will free the Cancerian from this 'life script' position, by putting them more in charge of their own life and releasing them from emotional dependence on other people.

VENUS IN LEO

If you have Venus in Leo, you will be loyal and affectionate in your relationships. You are likely to be fond of children and get on well with them.

In a love relationship you may put your partner on a pedestal, but you will also want to dominate. This tends to be true of most of your relationships. You can be a perfect friend, generous, unchanging, good-natured, as long as everyone recognises that you are the boss.

You need to be loved and appreciated and can be upset if this is lacking in your life. On these occasions you should consider whether the problem has been that you have become too overbearing for the other person to accept. Remember that you must concede other people's right to run their own lives. To feel that they *should* love you because you have been generous towards them is a form of bribery and they will not give you genuine love and friendship in return.

There is also a danger in having too much dignity to show your feelings. If someone has hurt you, it is much better to tell them, "I feel hurt because . . . ", than to keep it to yourself and continue to feel unloved.

A great deal of damage is done to relationships because people (not only Leos) will not be frank about their feelings. Many times this results in people being at cross-purposes with each other instead of being able to explain why a certain situation has occurred. People do not usually intend to hurt others, unless they are angry themselves, and are often surprised to learn that that has been the result of some thoughtless word or action. Remember that cross-purposes make cross people.

VENUS IN VIRGO

The person with Venus in Virgo has the critical attitude to others which the sun–Virgoan adopts toward him or herself. It is, perhaps, for this reason that many of them remain single.

In work conditions, they are not good at handling staff because they find it difficult to delegate. No-one's work is ever quite good enough so praise is rarely given. The Virgoan can treat insignificant faults as though they had caused a major crisis.

Nobody likes to be constantly criticised; not even the people who have learned how to treat it constructively. Consequently, the Virgoan is likely to find that friendships are difficult to keep intact and that people in close relationship are either resentful or have learnt to ignore the constant carping.

Despite this fault, which may suggest that the Virgoan thinks that *he* is perfect, they are truly rather shy and lacking in self-confidence, probably because they make too much of their own shortcomings. The result is that they are abnormally sensitive to criticism from others. They need to learn to build creatively from an experience of failure.

Virgoans are kind and helpful. In fact, they are so good-hearted that they will do anything for anyone, but like the Cancerians they cannot understand why other people are not the same to them and they are hurt when someone who has received help from them does not reciprocate.

Their emotional energy is low, but they blossom when they feel truly loved and appreciated. They need to be constantly reminded that we are all unique and that we are all fallible human beings and must learn to live with our failings.

VENUS IN LIBRA

Libra like Taurus, is ruled by Venus, so whether you have a Libra sun sign or Venus in Libra, you are likely to be Venusian. Relationships will be important to you, and in particular, partnerships. You are likely to spend a lot of time looking for 'the one and only' and may often imagine yourself in love.

Librans usually do well in relationships, business as well as personal, and they tend to get on well with colleagues. The tact and diplomacy which is fundamental to their natures results in them being generally popular.

They will shy away from anything in the nature of a quarrel and this can mean that they allow themselves to be manipulated by others. It takes a lot of courage for a Libran to face or instigate a confrontation, however necessary it may be.

Libra is one of the zodiac signs whose natives need to make it clear right from the beginning of a relationship that they will not let other people rule their lives, before a situation arises that calls for stronger resistance.

Venus in this sign is well placed for indicating happy marriages, but being an Air sign, Librans do need a partner who stimulates them mentally as well as physically. They can 'weigh' every little fault of the partner and easily throw the relationship 'off balance', so there may be many false starts before they decide to settle for a less-than-perfect partner. However, if they do not form a close relationship, they will always feel that their life is incomplete.

Like the Taureans, who are also ruled by Venus, the Libran may resent another person's good luck, and is quick to feel that 'it's not fair'. Unless they are aware of this tendency, they may develop into a whiner and this will affect all their relationships badly.

VENUS IN SCORPIO

If Venus is in Scorpio in your birth chart, you are also a person who needs to make your position clear to other people from the start. Not that you are likely to let them manipulate you for long, but you will resent it until you explode into anger instead of dealing with it before you reach that stage.

You are likely to be a passionate and highly emotional person (balanced, of course, if your sun and moon are not in Scorpio). You are easily hurt by others and are too concerned with what they will think of you. If you let it, this attitude can inhibit your actions much more than other people ever could.

You share with Taurus the ability to become jealous and possessive. Recognise this for what it is, the fear of losing someone you care for and you will realise, since you are clearminded, that no-one is worth keeping on those terms.

Most people are fascinated by the sheer power of the Scorpion and this may make some people fear them, while others are drawn to them, sensing a strength which they need. They may, therefore, find other people depending on them and loading them with responsibilities.

Although they are hurt by others, they can certainly hurt others in return, especially as they have a biting tongue. They often use sarcasm as a weapon and will not forget an injury.

Many of us, not only Scorpios, tend to relive past hurts, feeling the same emotions over and over again, thinking of retorts we might have made or wishing that we acted differently. There is no gain in this. The 'other person' has long since forgotten about it and the only person you are hurting is yourself. If you find yourself living in the past in this way, resolutely turn your mind to something positive. It is therapeutic to realise what a fool you have been to punish yourself like this. Do not give the other person the advantage, even if they never know it, of continuing to upset your life through a past action.

VENUS IN SAGITTARIUS

People whose birth chart shows Venus in Sagittarius will be idealistic in love. They need a partner who recognises that they cannot be 'fenced in' and they should be prepared to give that same freedom back.

Sagittarians are tolerant people and are free-and-easy in their friendships. They do not have much trouble in their personal relationships, but many of these will be casual and not have much depth to them.

In an effort to avoid responsibility, the Sagittarian can preclude any really close contact with others and may find themselves lonely in later life.

Colleagues, too, may resent their tendency to 'pass the buck' and although they will appreciate the Sagittarian easy and optimistic approach, they will regard them as 'light weight'. This is a pity, as they are capable of deep study and hard work, if a subject really grabs their interest.

Sagittarians have a likeable personality and most people warm to their friendliness and happy outlook on life.

Venus in Sagittarius is not strong. Among other things, Venus represents what we care about and how we are willing to cooperate with others. Sagittarians like to be footloose and do not want to cooperate. More than most, except Aquarius, they want to do their own thing.

Since this book is all about self-fulfilment, you may think the Sagittarian has already achieved it, but most people do not feel fulfilled if they are always alone. The Sagittarian can cope with loneliness better than most people but they are, after all, a Fire sign with an ardent nature. Like the rest of us, they want to love and be loved, but not fettered by emotional relationships.

VENUS IN CAPRICORN

When Venus is in Capricorn any relationships formed will be durable. Loyalty and responsibility both in friendships and in marriage will be likely.

The Capricornian (especially sun–Capricorn) is recognised as the typical father-figure and provider. All who have this sign strong in their birthcharts are likely to be fond of children and to appreciate a happy, stable home life. However, they will expect to be the king in their own castle.

Despite their wish for a happy home life, they tend to be rather cool in showing their feelings and as they are also quite strict there may be a 'generation gap', which is larger than usual between father and children.

The natural ambition of the Capricorn native may mean that they expect more from their children than is reasonable and they may also contract a marriage or make friendships which they think will help their own career or status.

Traditionally, those who have Venus in Capricorn often have to make sacrifices for others, or take on responsibilities in personal relationships. This can also

61

indicate marriage to someone considerably older (an authority figure).

Sometimes the native suffers from the coldness or strictness of others, especially his or her own father, but more often they suffer from their own disposition to keep emotions under strict control.

Colleagues may see them as reliable but cold, while those who love them may be hurt by their apparent inability to express their love in return.

VENUS IN AQUARIUS

Before the outer planets, Uranus, Neptune and Pluto, were discovered it was thought that Saturn was the ruler of Aquarius, as it is of Capricorn. Certainly the two signs have much in common, especially in the matter of relationships, where both are cool and detached.

Venus in Aquarius makes for friendly relationships and lots of them. The Aquarian likes to be a member of a club or society and will probably take an active part in it. As with Libra, another Air sign, there will be a desire to help everyone to obtain justice.

Both in friendship and in closer relationships, there will be a lack of warmth and emotional expression. If the sun sign is also Aquarius, or Capricorn, the best marriage partner is someone who does not require a demonstrative lover. The Water signs would be unsuitable for them unless they have a more emotional moon sign. The Aquarian makes a faithful and loyal friend and will do anything for anyone, but will not tolerate possessiveness.

VENUS IN PISCES

Although Venus does not rule Pisces it is said to be 'exalted' in that sign, meaning that it is free to express its attributes in the most positive way. The Piscean needs love and to give love in all their relationships. They want to be appreciated by their boss and liked by colleagues. With Venus in this sign, a happy love-life is almost guaranteed!

The desire to help others and to identify with people in trouble makes them suckers for a hard-luck story, but they can be oversentimental.

Their need for the reassurance of love makes Pisceans particularly vulnerable to manipulation. They can accept a life-script of 'the one who sacrifices for others', but what most of them sacrifice is their right to be themselves and they become what their partner wants them to be. A Piscean woman married to a man who encourages her to 'do her own thing' will be a totally different person from the one whose husband thinks a wife is a bed-mate, cook and child nurse and nothing else.

If you have been able to obtain your birthchart, you will know which house Venus is in, so here is a brief description of how Venus works through the houses.

House 1. This is the house of the personality, so even if you are not a Taurean or Libran, relationships will be of primary importance to you. You are likely to have charm of manner and get on well with most people. An ability to relax can become laziness.

House 2. Possessions are indicated here, and Venus in this position indicates a tendency to be possessive in relationships. It is, however, a good position for financial matters and business partnerships.

House 3. You value your immediate family, particularly brothers and sisters. You use words well and are likely to have an attractive speaking voice. You probably use your hands in an artistic way.

House 4. This is the house of the home, so if Venus is here, it is likely to be a happy one with loving relationships — that is what you would wish.

House 5. Creativity and children are emphasised here. You will value your relationships with your children, and sexual creativity will be important to you. A good position for all artistic pursuits.

House 6. The house of work and health. Venus here usually indicates good health and pleasant relationships with colleagues. If work conditions are not pleasant, health will suffer (see next chapter).

House 7. Venus in the house of partnerships — what could be better! There will be likelihood of making excellent marriages and also business partnerships. If a loving relationship is not formed you will feel unfulfilled and may express your frustration by being resentful.

House 8. This is a good position for harmonious sexual relationships and is also good financially, often from inheritance.

House 9. You will value education and enjoy life as a student. You can make good relationships with foreigners and may travel a lot, or settle down in another country.

House 10. The house of the career. Venus here brings the likelihood of a career in the arts, or as an agent between your employers and the general public. You will value public status.

House 11. You are likely to have many friends and work within societies or clubs to which you will bring diplomacy to maintain good relationships within the group.

House 12. You have a need for privacy in personal relationships, and may be required to keep other people's secrets as well as your own.

Mars is also important in close relationships. There are two reasons for this. The planet Mars represents the vitality and motivation in life. This can refer to sexual drive and a good Venus to Mars aspect is usually present in a healthy love partnership. But it is also important that the incentives of two people should be compatible, if they are hoping for a permanent liaison. A woman who has ambitions to reach a better standard of life and is willing to forward her husband's career is likely to become frustrated and disillusioned if she marries a man with Mars in Libra where motivation is weak and who is not really interested in achievement.

MARS IN THE ZODIAC

We shall deal with Mars more fully later, but this is a brief description of how it works in the signs in terms of incentive.

If Mars is in **Aries**, vitality will be good and the 'drive' in life is likely to be directed to furthering one's own interests. In this sign, there will be a strongly Martian and Arian personality, even if the sun is in another sign. Initiative and leadership are emphasised.

In **Taurus**, the incentive will be for possessions, with the object of feeling secure through ownership of the necessities and some of the luxuries of life. Sexual life is much enjoyed, but possessiveness needs to be kept within bounds.

Mars in **Gemini** is not strong, as in all the Air signs, and there will be a liking, rather than a strong urge, for plenty of variety.

If you have Mars in **Cancer**, your fundamental motivation will be to establish a home of your own. Family matters will always be the most important things in your life.

In **Leo**, the Martian drive will be directed to becoming the leader in whatever field interests you. Plenty of purposeful enthusiasm is assured.

Mars in **Virgo** directs the above-average energy into work situations. There are health hazards in this position which will be discussed in the next chapter. There is likely to be a strong drive to give service to others.

As already stated, Mars is weak in **Libra** and there will be a desire for a quiet, pleasant and relaxed life. Vitality may fluctuate.

In the days before we knew of the outer planets, it was thought that the ruler of **Scorpio** was Mars. It is certainly strong when positioned here. The incentive is to penetrate deeply into anything which arouses interest. Often this is some aspect of the occult. Sexual feelings are strong, but relationships can be ruined by jealousy.

In **Sagittarius**, Mars' incentive is for freedom of action. There is often a positive spur to self-fulfilment which can bring a rewarding life, provided the individual with Mars in Sagittarius makes sure that their partner is also encouraged to expand in this way.

When Mars is in **Capricorn**, it adds a vitality to the Capricornian's ambition, and life may be devoted to the attainment of power and status. Even when goals are more modest, there will be an incentive to succeed. Sometimes ambitions are for children to achieve and this can cause psychological difficulties for the children if unrealistic expectations are expressed.

Although those with the sun in **Aquarius** are more prone to preach revolution than to lead it, if Mars is in this sign such ideas are more likely to be put into practice. This can be disruptive, or it can be a conscious striving for humanitarian aims.

Mars in **Pisces** is likely to be expressed in self-sacrifice and working for others. If this is done on a conscious level, it can be rewarding. However, it sometimes results in the individual becoming the victim of their own generous instinct to help other people because they allow exploitation.

You will see from this short explanation that people whose life incentives are the same, or are compatible, start their relationship with a tremendous advantage. If you are already in a situation where your partner's idea of a satisfying life is not the same as your own, it will be necessary to consider whether either of you is prepared to change this and, if not, whether each can pursue their own goals within the relationship.

Self-fulfilment is likely to involve you in making major changes and these may be disruptive of close partnerships. If you have little in common, a break-up may be the best solution in the end. Alternatively, you might decide to settle for something less than complete autonomy in order to preserve the relationship. This must be your decision, made in *full appreciation of the situation*.

These salient five words are the key to happy relationships. If you appreciate the other person's situation as well as your own, you will nearly always find common ground, since we all have a deep-rooted need for each other. Anyone who thinks self-fulfilment means that each of us pursues his or her own aims in a purely selfish way is suffering from delusion. Union and love is the stuff of life itself and we cannot live without it. If we try to do so, we shall end up as psychological cripples.

So how does one begin to resolve a difficult relationship?

The first step is to really understand yourself and your own motivations — what makes you tick. A professional astrologer can help you with a character analysis from your birthchart. (Ways of finding properly qualified astrologers are given at the end of this book.)

From your birth chart you will know the position of Venus and Mars, as well as your sun sign and you will also know your Ascending sign, but this still leaves out a great deal which an astrologer would consider. As well as planets, there are the house positions and, in particular, the aspects (relationships) which planets make to each other. These can be either 'easy' or 'difficult'. Where two planets combine harmoniously — perhaps both are in a Fire sign — the facets of personality which they represent will cause no difficulty. With the sun and Venus in an 'easy' aspect, for instance, the basic personality (the sun) would be compatible with the attitude to personal relationships (Venus). Similarly if there is a 'difficult' aspect between the Ascendant and the moon, for example, the way that individuals project themselves (Ascendant) will not represent the way that they really feel (moon–emotions). In this case, other people may misjudge the individual. All the difficult aspects in the chart represent a challenge, but they can be resolved, if one is aware of them.

Many people make the mistake of assuming that a facet of their personality represents the real self.

'I am so sensitive', or, 'I am quick-tempered', are the kind of remarks which are frequently made, but the 'I' is much more than the sum of its parts. Suppose the sensitive person stopped being sensitive. Would he or she cease to exist? Of course not, rather they would begin to free their real self from the bondage of a habitual life-script.

On the stage, one can only take a part, one character in the play; but life is not like that. The essential 'I' is beyond all the characters which we may project — the victim, the sacrifice, the organiser, the critic, the invalid, or whatever role we choose to assume. Note that word *choose*. It was not used lightly.

I cannot emphasise too strongly that we all have the power to take charge of our own lives. If facets of life are not as you would wish, not only do you have the power to change them, but you also need to recognise that you yourself have contributed to their presence. In her book *Relating*, Dr Liz Greene says:

> Nothing comes into a man's life that is not a reflection of something within himself. Nothing is ever wholly the fault of another, for at the deepest roots of our being we are all one psyche, and the same life stream permeates us all.

Each of us has many of the saintly virtues and many of the criminal vices — but *we* are not those virtues or vices.

However, we must recognise that they are present in us whether obvious to all, or hidden even from ourselves.

We can all be helped to self-fulfilment, but we need to admit the possibility of change and we must *want to change*. Only if you think you are perfect can you inhibit your own inner growth to maturity.

Most of us recognise our faults, but we find excuses for them, often because we are aware of the feelings which caused them. But of course, there is no excuse for other people's faults, is there? We know how hard *we* have tried not to be revengeful, sarcastic or hurtful, so we tend to say, "I let it pass at first, but that was the last straw." If our constant nagging is 'the last straw' for someone else, we don't know that and only feel that we have been hurt without provocation.

Many people who learn a little about astrology think that they have a perfect excuse: "I can't help being quick-tempered. I've got Mars in Aries." "My sun gets bad aspects from Saturn so naturally

I seem cold to others." "I've got a strong Virgo, so I criticise even when I don't mean it."

Sorry. That's one thing astrology won't do. You can't blame your inadequacies on your birthchart. Neither 'the stars', nor anyone, nor anything can force you to do something against your will.

I was once in an encounter group where a young man (we'll call him Peter) had admitted that he had been suicidal at times in his life. This is how the conversation continued:

> *Therapist.* How do you feel now? Do you want to kill yourself?
> *Peter.* Hell, no! I want to live.
> *Therapist.* OK. So, let's make a contract. I'll help you if you will promise not to kill yourself. Say it.
> *Peter* (slowly). Well, of course I don't want to kill myself . . .
> *Therapist.* OK. Then say it. "Whatever happens I won't kill myself."
> (Peter avoided saying the actual words after the therapist had had several attempts at getting him to commit himself.)
> *Therapist.* Well, I certainly admire you.
> *Peter.* What's to admire?
> *Therapist.* Your determination. You are still clinging to the idea that if things get rough, suicide is always a get-out.
> *Peter.* Yes. It feels like a life-line.
> *Therapist* (shaking his head). Suicide feels like a life-line, but you know it's a death-line don't you?

Peter did, but he wasn't to be shaken, at least, not on that occasion, not even for his own good. This is how much we stubbornly cling to our own favourite 'bad feelings'.

What is *your* favourite way of coping with difficulties? Retreat? Explosion? Apparently reacting coolly while churning inside? Whatever it is, try to imagine that you have been forbidden to use that particular method. Scary, isn't it? The unknown is always frightening until it becomes familiar by repeated acquaintance with it. We shall talk about methods of overcoming fear of the unknown later.

We have already seen that the first step to improving relationships is to become more aware of our needs, our expectations and our present difficulties and to start work on solving them.

The second step is to understand that other people have similar needs, expectations and difficulties — not exactly the same, but comparable enough for us to understand each other.

In any relationship, the most frequent cause of trouble is simply misunderstanding the other person's words, actions or feelings. Many of us are not clever at using words precisely enough to convey an exact meaning; some of our actions conceal our real feelings, as in the person who copes coolly with a crisis while actually being frightened. We all tend to inhibit our feelings since we have been taught to believe that it is not adult to express them fully.

I have found it helpful in analysing what people are *really* conveying (which may have little to do with the words they actually use) to visualise the personality as three separate identities. This is a method used in a type of psychotherapy known as Transactional Analysis.

Each person consists of a Parent, Adult and Child. Capital letters are used for these because they do not mean precisely what would normally be meant by the words.

The Parent is the part of us which is parental to others and can be a Nurturing Parent ('Let me help you with that'), or a Critical Parent ('You shouldn't do that'). The Critical Parent contains all our prejudices. For instance, our own parents may have taught us, 'All employers are exploiters'.

The Child part of us, the moon in astrology, is the part which is free to express emotions and to state exactly how we feel. People at a party who are relaxed together and are having fun are in their 'Free Child' personality. There is also an 'Adapted Child', who responds to the parent by conforming to parental injunctions. This is the emotional part of us which causes hang-ups.

But there is also an Adult. This is free from emotion and from parental nurturing or prejudice. We see it operating in work situations where the individual is busy dealing with data and processing it in some way. A secretary who is taking dictation is concentrating on the matter and is not normally conscious of anything but the task of the moment. In practice, she may switch her attention to her annoyance at her employer's dithering (Critical Parent), or her own feelings of anxiety about something personal (Child). But while she is completely involved in the job, she is functioning in the Adult, which can be compared with a computer receiving data and working on it.

This is a most valuable part of the personality for problem solving. If there is difficulty in a relationship, we are not likely to help matters if we are in our Critical Parent and attempt to judge the other person according to our own prejudices. Nor does it help to be all emotion at such times, as our own strong feelings will prevent us from seeing where the real difficulty lies. If we can 'stay in the Adult' we will accomplish several things. Firstly, we will prevent ourselves feeling the emotion which we might normally feel in an argument. This is not the same as suppressing the emotion. One actually ceases to feel it. Staying in the Adult makes us cool and detached. If we can do this, we remain in charge of the situation. Secondly, such an approach may help the other person to respond from their Adult so that difficulties can be discussed reasonably. Thirdly, if the other person is not willing to respond in this way and continues to operate from the Critical Parent or Adapted Child, in an effort to manipulate us, they will fail.

Here are a few examples of how this might work out in practice. Every exchange in conversation is a transaction and we will analyse these to see which facet of the personality is involved in each.

Example 1. Husband to wife, "What's the time?" Wife replies, "Heavens, aren't you ready yet? You'll miss the train again." Here is a diagram to show this situation.

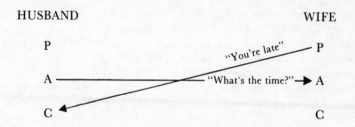

Illustration of a crossed transaction (P parent, A adult, C child)

The husband spoke from his Adult and expected an Adult response. The wife replied as a Critical Parent, to the Adapted Child in her husband, giving him a 'put down'. This is known as a 'crossed transaction' and once this has occurred it precludes the possibility of further rational conversation.

71

Example 2. Two men are discussing politics. They are both members of the same political party and are quite happily criticising all the policies of the opposition. The chances are that they are both in their Critical Parent, but you can see from the diagram on page 71 that the lines would be going straight across the page from Parent to Parent, so there is no crossed transaction and the conversation can go on for a long time.

Example 3. A child comes home in tears, saying that he feels ill. Mother replies that she will give him a hot drink and get him to bed. Here the child is in the Free Child (showing his feelings simply) and is appealing to the Nurturing Parent. The mother responds from her Nurturing Parent to the Child. Again there is no crossed transaction.

Example 4. In a work situation a man asks, "Are we out of forms X? I can't find any." His colleague replies, "Yes. I ordered some last week, but they haven't come yet." Here, both are plainly in the Adult. No emotion of any sort is involved.

Example 5. A couple are in the middle of an argument which they have often had before. She says, "You make a scene every time I need money, but you spend all you want on yourself." Suddenly, as he is about to retort angrily, the man sees what he should do and replies calmly, "Look, let's sit down and work out our present budget and see if we can improve it." She is probably switching from Critical Parent to Adapted Child (complaining and perhaps crying), as the argument proceeds. He has been doing the same, but his sudden switch to Adult makes a crossed transaction, puts him in charge of the situation and makes it impossible for her to continue the argument. If she tries, he should 'stay in the Adult' by responding reasonably or refusing to argue.

Of course, it often happens that trouble in relationships goes deeper than this and that the complaint which is voiced is not the one which is causing the difficulty. In this case, counsellors can often be helpful. However, if the situation is not serious and both parties understand Transactional Analysis, the beginning of an argument can often be stopped as one replies from the Adult and the other then realises what they are doing. The man who told his wife that he was not responsible for her guilty feelings was a case in point. Her Adapted Child, apologising for not helping him with the dishes, was appealing to his Nurturing Parent not to be cross with her. His reply made her realise this and she stopped feeling guilty.

If you have had a lot of difficulty with relationships and have experienced the feeling of being 'put down' often, I can promise you that learning to 'stay in your Adult' is a giant step towards self-fulfilment. You need to realise that your favourite bad feeling is a habit, just like any other and that it will take time to break the habit of feeling put-down. But every time you can get into the Adult, you experience the freedom of being in charge of the situation and that makes it easier to do the same thing again. Gradually you learn to handle all these difficulties and wonder why you ever let other people make you feel bad.

Of course, the Adult is cold, being devoid of emotion and in a close relationship a hug from the Free Child may be more appropriate and certainly more enjoyable. Do not think that it is wrong to use all the parts of the personality, as each has its value. (See Appendix 2 for further reading on Transactional Analysis.)

In her book, *Synastry*, Penny Thornton says that we get the relationships we deserve and certainly we need to work on ourselves to see where we fall short. Recently, I saw a televised documentary in which a class of school girls was being asked about a choice of career. One girl said that she wanted to marry and have her family while she was young. The teacher nodded understandingly, but asked, "And what do you have to bring to the relationship?" The girl's jaw dropped and she stared in blank amazement. It was easy to see that it had never occurred to her that such a common thing as marriage needed a genuine contribution from both partners.

In this type of close involvement, there needs to be compatibility in aims and emotions. There will always be some fundamental feelings which will preclude us from making good relationships with everyone and these we will need to keep on a superficial level. ('If we find each other, its beautiful. If not it can't be helped.' Remember?). A long-standing friendship will never grow closer if one is always a giver and the other always a taker (unless the giver *wants* to sacrifice himself, which would not be a healthy situation). The taker may express love but the giver will always wonder if it is genuine, since most lovers want to give.

The person who knows he or she needs reassurance of love is asking for trouble if a partner is chosen who is cold-natured or undemonstrative. The one who needs a great deal of personal freedom should not marry someone who clings.

But we already know that we cannot be fitted into any one category, so let an astrologer help you to understand yourself and those who matter to you. In particular, if you are contemplating a permanent relationship (business, marriage, sharing a house), ask an astrologer to compare your birth charts and tell you if you are suitable partners for the object you have in mind. Here are two examples of the types of situations where this has proven to be helpful.

Example 1. A widow who owned an antique shop considered taking into partnership a friend who often helped her when she was busy. A comparison of their charts showed that the widow was a meticulous person. The shop always looked attractive and was kept spotless. The friend had a great flair for valuing goods but was very untidy. When this was pointed out to them, they agreed to carry on as they were, instead of possibly putting the friendship at risk by entering into a formal partnership.

Example 2. A young couple are in love and intend to marry. The charts show that they are compatible emotionally, but the astrologer sees one major difficulty. The young woman is completely home-oriented. Most of her planets are in Cancer and around the fourth house. Her fiancé's chart shows much wider interests and reveals the possibility of a spectacular career involving travel abroad, perhaps for long periods. The astrologer explains this and asks the young woman, "Are you going to stay at home if your husband has to go away, or will you accompany him?" The girl feels quite shattered at the time but later decides she will accompany her husband whenever she can and thanks the astrologer for giving her the opportunity to decide before the situation arises.

Astrology can also be helpful where a partnership has been good but starts to go wrong, perhaps through financial difficulties, ill-health or the interference of a third party. The astrologer not only looks at the relevant birth charts, but also considers the present position. This invloves a technique known as 'progressions', the chart being progressed to bring it up to date. From this technique future forecasts may be made. It is rarely possible for an astrologer to be able to state categorically that on a certain date a certain event will occur, but it is certainly possible to see the present and future trends. The astrologer may then be able to tell the couple how long the difficult situation is likely to last. If they are reassured that they are well suited to each other, almost all couples decide to stay together and weather the difficulties.

For many couples, difficulties serve to cement bonds of love more strongly and there is no question of a break in their relationship, but even they may appreciate guidance as to how long their particular trouble is likely to last.

Close, intimate relationships are not the only form of human contact that need to be developed. Business colleagues, friends and acquaintances are all worth cultivating, not least for the reason that a relationship may lead to another more important one.

Why are you friendly with this person and dislike that one? Is it because all your friends must agree with your ideas? If so, you are closing yourself to many experiences. Try not to judge if any new idea is valid until you have tested it in some way. For instance, if the validity of astrology is in question, no-one should pronounce on it unless they have attended a serious lecture or read a book on the subject and had their own birth chart interpreted by a competent astrologer. If you are asked for a judgement on a matter on which you know nothing, you will find that to say, "I have an open mind on it, because I have never investigated it", will do you no harm at all with sensible people.

If you can accept and like people who are different from yourself and come from a different background, not only will your circle of friends expand, but also you will be enriched by being exposed to experiences which many people do not have. A few years ago, I attended an Indian wedding and was lucky enough to have all the symbolism explained to me. It made me aware of the cultural differences, but it also showed me the inner wisdom of some of them.

We tend to be conditioned by our experience of past relationships. Old friends have often shared experiences which hold them together. Wartime comrades become friends for life, for no better reason than that they have known each other in circumstances where class, rank and background failed to be important.

During the Second World War, a Jewish corporal had his home in the poor quarter of London destroyed. His captain arranged for his wife and family to stay with his own wife in the north of England and the two families found so much in common that the Jewish family moved to the northern town after the war just to be near their friends. They had discovered that their *values* were the same, despite having different backgrounds.

If you are shy with people you can learn to be more forthcoming by taking a genuine interest in their hobbies or work. If you learn how to draw people out on their own subject you will find that most of them can be fascinating. An expert describing his discipline with enthusiasm can usually hold an audience spellbound — and most of us are experts on (or enthusiastic about) something. Remember to maintain eye contact, because it shows that you are giving others your full attention. You will soon find that you become popular, for everyone loves a good listener.

Physical gestures can help immensely. We often fail to show people that we find them attractive, fearing that we may be rebuffed. It is always worth making the attempt. After all, a rebuff does no more than hurt your pride temporarily, whereas acceptance can gain you a friend for life. So take courage and offer that warm handshake, or a hug. If your gesture is not met wholeheartedly, the loss is theirs, not yours.

We continue to need a maternal type of love and affection all our lives. You know this is true of yourself, so accept that it is true of everyone else, even though they may not show it. Lack of nurture is not fatal, but those who can provide it just when it is most needed will never lack friends. I am not talking about being overprotective and certainly one should not encourage people to be sorry for themselves, but there are times of genuine bereavement or loss when everyone needs a shoulder to cry on.

Above all, value your friends. People are unpredictable, so you never come to the end of knowing them and this is life-enhancing. Extend your circle, don't limit yourself to just a few.

Readiness to cooperate with others implies that we recognise the need for compromise, a Venusian concept, symbolised by the sign of Libra. If you are short on diplomacy, recognise the fact and you are on your way to curing it.

Even more than the shy person, the one who is most likely to lack genuine friends is the person who is so self-absorbed that they only see conditions as they affect them and believe that their wishes are paramount, not only to themselves, but to everyone.

Once, a young niece and her husband who were coming to stay with me for a weekend, asked if they could bring a friend of theirs who was due to compete in a boat race near to where we lived, as this would save him an early morning journey from Oxford to London. We agreed and expected to provide him with dinner, bed and breakfast. Instead of being duly grateful, the young man expressed himself very forcibly because the meals I provided were unsuitable for his training. I think he left without any breakfast at all. The night before, he had dominated the conversation with talk about himself (but failed to mention his diet, when I might have been able to do something about it) and generally gave the impression that he expected the world to revolve around him. I cannot imagine that anyone would want to give him hospitality again. Such a person is usually functioning in their moon sign which relates to childhood and emotions. Most of us learn, either from our parents or from life, that we have to consider others, but some people never grow up. If the young man had been a cosseted only child whose parents had fostered his belief that he was all important, it is not surprising that he was taking a long time to learn otherwise.

I cannot leave this chapter without reiterating that all our relationships ought to be equal partnerships. It is fatally easy to let another person's expectations dominate you. I would like to recount two true stories. A young woman of my acquaintance felt that she must fulfil her parent's expectations that she should marry. In due course, she became engaged to a young man from her own group of university friends. Her parents were delighted and planned a big wedding. Before it took place, she started to realise that she and her fiancé had little in common and rarely went out together, except as part of a group. Because of the wedding preparations, which were now well advanced, she felt compelled to go through with it rather than face up to her parents' reactions. The inevitable result was a divorce two years later and, of course, the parents said, "If only she had told us how she felt."

The other story has a happier ending. A young woman came to me with a problem. She had met a former fiancé and they had found that they still loved each other. Both were engaged to other people and did not want to hurt them. I do not believe in telling people what to do, so I simply said, "What is the alternative? Perhaps as long as fifty years with the wrong man?" It was enough. As she said afterwards, "That concentrated my mind wonderfully." When she told her present fiancé, he was shattered for a while, but was able to write to her later, "I know you well enough to appreciate that it took some courage to tell me, but you wouldn't have been doing me any favours if you had married me feeling as you did. How could we have been happy? This way, I do have a chance of happiness with someone else."

If issues are important enough, frankness always pays. It can be done gently, tactfully, even with expressions of regret, if appropriate, but it should be done. Muddles, hurt feelings and even wrong decisions occur when facts are concealed and your genuine feelings are facts, just like anything else.

Love between partners is our most important and most complex relationship. It involves all that we are, Parent, Adult and Child, and that extra quality of the spirit which is also a component of the essential self. No wonder that it is fraught with difficulty, but it is also well worth working at for the reward is great; no less than constant nourishment to self-development and the life of the individual.

5
HEALTH AND VITALITY

Ill-health can be a major difficulty on the path to self-fulfilment, but it is not an insuperable obstacle. This book is dedicated to a brilliant man who was struck down with crippling disease at the age of 25 and who never regained the full use of his back and legs. He got around with sticks, painfully and slowly, but he never let that stop him doing what he wanted to do. He lectured as far afield as India, as well as America and Europe, and his wise and loving spirit was a blessing to all who knew him. He was a dedicated teacher to severely handicapped children, who must surely have been inspired by his example. His work for astrology has still to be evaluated, but it was outstanding. He had a lively sense of humour and a wicked way with words — no 'stiff upper lip', or 'look how brave I am being' attitude to his disability. He simply ignored it.

His disease would appear to have been unavoidable, but this is far from being true of most illness. On the contrary many doctors would agree that 80 per cent of them are psychosomatic. That does not mean that they are imaginary, but it does mean that an illness can originate in the mind, even though it manifests physical symptoms.

I have written elsewhere of complementary medicine* (as distinct from orthodox drug-based medicine) and therapies which may suit each of the zodiacal types and help to relieve symptoms. In this chapter I want to draw attention to the ways in which we can cause our own illnesses.

One of the greatest killers in our present busy world is stress. Like many other things, it is good in small doses, but when it becomes permanent tension, the nervous system reacts critically, resulting in what we call a breakdown. But this is only one of the causes which can trigger the symptoms of ill-health. You may be surprised to learn that these include such conditions as boredom, self-centredness, resentment, frustration and fears of all kinds, as

---

Astrology and Health (see appendix)

well as unhealthy regimes. For this reason, the birth chart, which shows the psychological make-up, can be a great help in showing *what we can do to ourselves* to cause ill-health.

Some people stay ill to avoid unpleasant situations, to postpone decisions for fear of failure ("If I'm not well enough to take the exam, I can't fail it"), or to get attention. These will not have been conscious actions, but are the result of deep, unconscious feelings. The road to self-fulfilment enables one to cope with all these situations with consequent improvement in health.

As Mars is the planet which indicates vitality, much can be judged from the sign in which it appears in the birth chart, but in the case of health conditions, the whole chart needs to be studied. In reading the descriptions for each sign, remember that the sun and moon also have much to do with health; the sun as the power point in the chart and the moon as the emotions.

A planet which we have not yet considered is Mercury. This planet refers to the thought patterns and also rules the nervous system. Since mental outlook has much to do with health, as has the nervous system, Mercury is important when examining a chart for health conditions.

HEALTH AND THE FIRE SIGNS

All the Fire signs have a lot of energy and vitality and they tend to spend it recklessly. With Mars in a Fire sign, this can result in accidents, fevers and over-activity of the vital organs.

In **Aries**, this tendency is particularly strong, as it is ruled by Mars. If you have Mars in its own sign, you will be a very Arien personality, even though the sun and moon are in other signs. Traditionally, Aries rules the head, the cerebral system and the adrenal glands. Words like headfirst and headlong are appropriate here, for the Arien tends to rush without looking — one reason why they are accident-prone — and erupts quickly into action or passion. They have a dynamic and vital personality and, on the whole, are not subject to psychosomatic illness because they do not brood over things. An above-average vitality is a mixed blessing as they tend to overtax both mind and body and overestimate their physical power to cope.

Being self-orientated, Ariens make a great fuss when anything trivial is wrong with them. They find it so frustrating to be prevented from getting on with their projects. But their great courage enables them to ignore serious disabilities so that they are a good example to all the hypochondriacs of the zodiac.

They are prone to headaches, migraines and fevers and need to learn to relax both in mind and body.

For all of us, our job in life absorbs a great deal of time, so a choice of suitable work can contribute greatly to the individual's well-being. Equally, work conditions which make us unhappy can subscribe to ill-health.

The Arien who has powers of leadership must be in a position where this energy and initiative can be used. If this is not possible in work conditions, a hobby should be found which will enable them to be fulfilled in this way.

The second Fire sign, **Leo**, is a powerful and vital sign in its own right, so if Mars is in this position great vitality can again be expected, though it will be used in a more practical way. Usually, this is an excellent position for good health. Leo is not afraid of taking responsibility for large projects and the typical picture of Leo is as the entrepreneur. In such a position they may overdrive and exhaust themselves and become prime candidates for a a coronary attack. This is the number one disease of the business person and it is caused by just such stress as Leo natives inflict upon themselves. It is, therefore, completely *avoidable*.

When either sun or Mars is in Leo, there will be courage, optimism and pride. In work conditions, these characteristics may lead the native to overestimate the amount that he or she can do — and then do it anyway. If they are too proud to ask for help, the pressure may become more than they can bear, in which case something has to give. Leo is associated with the heart and spine, so if a coronary is avoided there may be back trouble. Nature will revenge herself somehow if the body is continuously abused, in order to ensure that rest is enforced.

Anyone who is aware that they constantly put themselves under pressure only needs to take adequate rest and relaxation to avoid such illnesses. The relaxation should include exercise, as a great deal of mental stress in work conditions can be relieved by physical exercise.

Leo types are often fond of drama and this is excellent therapy for such people, enabling them to express emotions freely. As a result, most of them do not suffer from mental or emotional difficulties. However, the ability to conceal feelings behind the actor's mask may mean that they are inhibited from sharing their troubles with anyone else. Leo is one of the most masculine signs and feels that 'he' ought to be man enough to bear his troubles by himself. Recognition of this characteristic and a resolve to ask for help when it is needed should ensure that there are no major health difficulties.

The last of the Fire signs, **Sagittarius**, being happy-go-lucky and mentally relaxed, is usually free of psychologically induced illnesses.

The exception occurs when they feel trapped by conditions from which they cannot escape. Illness can then be a way of opting out. This does not happen often, as Sagittarians are good at taking avoiding action if they see such a circumstance arising.

Tiredness is usually mental and is caused by boredom, which is the great enemy of these people who need the stimulation of a challenge.

Mars in this sign will give an even greater impact to the Sagittarian's energy and enthusiasm and some of this needs to be dissipated in physical exercise. More than any of the other zodiacal types, this one must get out into the open air if they are to keep fit. Many Sagittarians enjoy working in the open, especially if the work is connected with sport or animals.

The traditional careers for these people include the priesthood, the legal profession and philosophy. All of these are likely to be occupations where there is some degree of self-employment and this would be appropriate so that the Sagittarian can be free of restrictions imposed by others.

If such work is not possible, it becomes even more necessary that the Sagittarian should take an interest in competitive sport as a hobby.

This sign is associated with the hips, thighs and liver. The hips and thighs can be kept mobile by the appropriate exercises or sports and the liver will be healthy if it is not upset by over-indulgence in the rich foods which the Sagittarian so often prefers.

After exercise, both mental and physical relaxation are necessary. Mental relaxation is particularly important if Mercury is in Sagittarius, as the mind and the nervous system will then be restless and continually seek intellectual challenges.

All the Fire signs need to know when to stop. They all live life to the full and forget that the body needs to relax. If they become ill, they tend to put off seeking help on the grounds that they are too busy, the very reason which is often the cause of the illness.

HEALTH AND THE EARTH SIGNS

The Earth signs tend to contract ailments which are associated with coldness and rigidity and which inhibit movement. These are nearly always psychosomatic and, therefore, *avoidable*. All of the three Earth signs can be obstinate and it is not a coincidence that 'stiff-necked' has two meanings; a rigid body is often caused by a rigid mind. By the same token, they are durable and many of them are healthy and long-lived.

Taurus receives a great deal of strength from the earth itself, and needs to renew links with nature whenever possible. Gardening, flower-arranging and walking in the country are all therapeutic. Taureans have lots of endurance and patience and enjoy taking their time to do things properly. They also like their comforts and overemphasis of their natural characteristics can make them lazy and self-indulgent. If they get too little exercise and too much good food and wine, their normally strong constitution will suffer.

Taurus governs the neck, throat and thyroid glands. There is a tendency for Taureans to build up tensions at the back of the neck (atlas and axis bones) and some gentle neck exercises or massage can be helpful.

Work needs to be something which will produce concrete results. Taureans want to see something positive, an end product, as the fruit of their labours, even if it is only a balance sheet. They have a flair for finance but should not go into a high-risk business, which would worry them far too much.

The need for security is equally important for them in their personal relationships, hence their tendency to jealousy and possessiveness. This can cause psychosomatic problems. With the unconscious desire to hang on to a relationship at all costs, the Taurean may become ill in an attempt to blackmail the partner into staying. This type of induced illness is not conscious, but it can manifest as a physical condition of restricted movement. This needs the help of a psychologist or counsellor rather than a doctor.

If Mars is in Taurus, firmness may easily become obstinacy, which, in itself, can generate bodily tension. Taureans tend to be pessimistic about their illnesses and do not contribute much to their own recovery, as they are likely to go against medical advice if they think that they know best. Luckily, most of them have strong constitutions and heal well.

Virgo is ruled by Mercury. In addition to the practical nature of the Earth type, there is the rather nervous Mercury pattern which shows itself as a general fussiness. Virgoans deplete their energy by the sheer amount of effort put into each detail. They are the typical workaholics and if Mars is in this sign its practical ability is likely to show itself by an itch to take over everyone else's jobs. Mars in this sign creates above average energy and is capable of very hard work, taking long working hours in its stride and feeling that everyone else is lazy if they cannot do likewise. A great deal of frustration is built up, both with other people's incompetence and with themselves if they cannot achieve the high standard which they set themselves.

All the Earth signs have a lot of 'stickability' and the Virgoan will go on and on in an effort to do the impossible. They need to recognise this characteristic and to learn to stop and evaluate whether or not a project is worthwhile at such a cost of time and energy.

They need to be able to complete each day's work in that day and should not go into professions where they may be constantly coping with a backlog of work, as this would worry them far too much. They find it difficult to relax and will not sleep if they go to bed with any problems on their minds. Any career which calls for precision will appeal to them, and they like office routine.

Virgo rules the abdomen and intestines and worry brings digestive troubles of all types and tension which may restrict movement. Many Virgoans are interested in health and diets and they certainly need to eat natural foods. They also need muscular exercise to preserve movement. They must learn to relax and, in particular, to relax the mind. Meditation techniques which enable them to do this are helpful to Virgoans.

They can be health fanatics and the slightest illness can concentrate their minds wonderfully, to the exclusion of all else. Consequently, they can become hypochondriacs unless they are aware of this and learn to turn their minds to other things.

It is amazing how often an illness or pain can be forgotten and eventually disappear if the mind is fully occupied with something else. The body is a great healer left to its own natural resources, but we often impede its recovery by adding our own worry and tension to the situation. This is especially true of the Virgoan.

Capricorn has a double dose of rigidity. It is ruled by Saturn, the planet of responsibility and discipline, as well as being an Earth sign. The Capricornian is a worrier and easily becomes tense. In work situations they can be overconscientious and dogmatic.

Like all the Earth types, they need to feel that their positions are secure, especially in the field of the career. Mars in this sign indicates strong ambitions to obtain positions of power. Success becomes all-important, but often initiates tensions. However, tension-induced illness is most likely to be caused by the inability to express emotions. Under pressure, the person with Mars in Capricorn may become quickly irritable, but will never explode into anger.

Capricorn is associated with the bones and skeletal system, especially the knees and the teeth. The tendency to suffer from colds, rheumatism and rigidity with consequent loss of movement is typical. Capricornians can also build up toxins which cause skin troubles. A great many of their physical difficulties are psychosomatic and could be prevented if they had an outlet for their emotions, such as music or painting.

Exercises which preserve movement and get the

circulation of the blood moving more rapidly are valuable to Capricornians.

Relaxation should be fun and should allow the free expression of the personality, the 'giddy goat' side, as well as the serious side. They tend to neglect themselves by suppressing or refusing to admit their symptoms, but Capricornians are tough and usually live longer than the other zodiacal types.

HEALTH AND THE AIR SIGNS

The Air signs emphasise the lungs and the nerves, so restlessness is a common characteristic. The sensitive nervous system shrinks from all unpleasantness and sometimes uses illness as a convenient way of escape. This means that many of their health troubles are psychosomatic and therefore *avoidable*.

Gemini is ruled by Mercury. The Geminian mercurial temperament can mean that they are rather nervously 'on the go' all the time. They live in a world of movement, hate being tied down and really need variety. Like their opposite number, Sagittarius, they can become ill through sheer boredom, so they do need a career which they find interesting and which stimulates their lively minds.

Mercury in Gemini overemphasises the mental and physical activity and the result is likely to be nervous exhaustion and nerve troubles generally, so it is important that the native should get enough relaxation, both physical and mental.

Gemini is associated with the hands, arms, shoulders, lungs and nervous system. Muscular restrictions across the shoulders may result from work conditions, typing for instance, and these can be prevented by shoulder-shrugging and gentle neck exercises at intervals during the day.

Any tensions which Geminians allow to build up may cause similar difficulties.

The chief cause of psychosomatic illness for these people is the feeling of being threatened or hemmed-in by restrictive conditions. For instance, asthma is recognised as a self-induced illness, caused by nerves and undue sensitivity.

If Mars is in Gemini, energy may be dissipated by too much activity causing exhaustion, but restlessness is also a big factor which means that relaxation can be difficult. Yoga exercises are often helpful to the Geminian.

Libra is the most sensitive of all the zodiacal characters. They really do get distressed by circumstances which other people would take in their stride. Mothers of Libran children will know that they become physically sick if they have a teacher who they dislike or are forced to study a subject which they find difficult.

Because they are so resentful of unfairness, they can brood upon their wrongs and carry a sense of grievance to unjustifiable lengths. This can engender many types of psychosomatic illness, which may also be caused by the Libran's wish to avoid making crucial decisions. They are not good at decision-making and will be quickly upset if they are forced into the position of having to come down on one side or the other.

It follows that they should be careful to find congenial employment. They often do well in self-employment or in a business partnership. Mars in this sign indicates energy fluctuation and often there is not a great deal of enthusiasm for a career. Mars is at its weakest in this sign, so drive and vitality may be lacking. In this case, pleasant jobs in the luxury trades, even if not well paid, could be the most sensible choice.

Libra is associated with the kidneys and lumbar area. Librans respond well to a balanced diet and in particular to a good balance between alkalis and acids. They need daily exercises which should be part of their routine as they can easily get lazy.

On the whole, Librans are good at maintaining balance and are one of the healthiest signs of the zodiac.

Restlessness and a constant desire for change are common traits with **Aquarians** and this will be emphasised if Mars is in this sign, perhaps inducing the native to become a revolutionary instead of just having revolutionary ideas. Although Aquarians can usually cope with being 'the only one in step', it can be exhausting to be in conflict with the Establishment all the time and this may result in blood pressure related illness.

Aquarius is associated with the circulatory system, as well as the shins and ankles. The native tends to suffer from varicose veins, swollen ankles and muscular cramps; all of which express the sense of constriction, the idea of something being held in tight which may eventually explode.

Like the Capricornian, they find it difficult to express emotions and their fundamental needs for freedom make them shrink from close relationships. For the same reason, they cannot tolerate conditions in which they feel restricted.

Being innovators with inventive minds, they are particularly good in a career where they have plenty of freedom to 'do their own thing'. If Mercury is in this sign, the nature is likely to be interested in modern science and many Aquarians are found working in television, often producing their own programmes. They have plenty of discipline to bring to such careers, provided they are not restricted by others.

They need fairly strenuous exercise in the open air to help the circulation and for the same reason it is important that they learn to breathe properly.

Like the Geminian, they need mental relaxation and should particularly avoid mental stimulation before bed time as they need a lot of sleep.

Psychosomatic illness can be a form of escape from conditions which they find restricting. An understanding of their own attitude to freedom and a realistic appreciation of how much is possible in their particular circumstances can be extremely helpful.

HEALTH AND THE WATER SIGNS

The Water signs are the ones who are most sensible about their health and will seek help as soon as it is required. An over-emphasis of this trait means that they can easily become hypochondriacs. Because they worry so much and are emotionally sensitive, they quickly become fearful and suspicious, so many of their illnesses are psychosomatic and — yes — *avoidable*.

Cancer is the worrier of the zodiac. Cancerians assume the protector or mother role and become overconcerned about other people, fussing unnecessarily about situations which do not really concern them. Their moods fluctuate quickly from elation to depression. They are well when they feel 'on top of the world' and soon get ill (imaginary, but it quickly becomes reality) if they are depressed.

Because they are over-quick to imagine slights or rejections, they will brood over past hurts, real or imaginary, and make themselves thoroughly depressed, instead of keeping the mind busy and cheerful.

Mars in this sign heightens emotional tension and the native may become upset or bad tempered quickly. Mercury here will emphasise the tendency to live in the past, which may lead to acute depression.

Cancer is associated with the breasts, stomach and alimentary canal. Worry and tension affect these parts of the body causing indigestion, ulcers, gastritis, etc., all of them psychosomatic.

All the Water signs have to battle with problems of weight. This is partly a fluid-retention difficulty, but is aggravated by their love of food. Their rate of metabolism is low and they require less nourishment than the other zodiacal signs, so they do not have to over eat in order to put on weight. The Cancerian is particularly at risk because both sexes enjoy cooking (perhaps even more than eating) and cannot resist trying new recipes. Natural foods and plenty of exercise will help this problem.

Careers for Cancerians which involve looking after people are suitable (nursing, catering, etc.) provided they do not take their jobs home with them, worrying about their patients or clients in their own time. Their interest in the past can be turned to good use in careers connected with this, such as antique dealing, or as a historian or researcher.

The sure way for Cancerians to keep well is for them to keep their minds lively and occupied.

Scorpio is the most intense sign of the zodiac. Calm and controlled on the surface, there is a strong, passionate driving force at work and the effort needed to keep this in bounds engenders tension.

Mars in this sign is strong and is a force for good in many ways but it does emphasise those deep emotions and if they are too rigidly controlled, health may suffer. Mercury here is generally good, the nervous system being strong.

Scorpios may overindulge in food and drink as a compensation for any of their troubles and this can cause illness as their bodies do not take kindly to highly spiced foods or stimulants.

This sign governs the throat and nasal passages, the pelvis, the reproductive system and the prostate gland.

Psychosomatic illnesses are caused by over sensitivity to the opinions of others which sometimes prevents them from making changes which they know need to be made, in case other people would not approve (like the manager of the shoe shop described on page 42). Scorpios seem to fear to express strong emotions, especially anger, as they feel that their reactions might become ungovernable, precisely what happens if they suppress their feelings for too long. This is a common dilemma with many zodiacal types, especially between parents and children, and ways of dealing with it will be discussed later.

Scorpios can be unreasonably suspicious of other people and get depressed for no good reason. They need mental relaxation and would find a creative hobby helpful.

These people have plenty of physical courage and often enjoy competitive sports which will provide the exercise they need.

Pisces has a double dose of sensitivity and often 'knows' intuitively when something is wrong with another member of the family. They have a dread of anything which means trouble; illness, arguments, or even house repairs, so that, although they do often possess this 'mediumistic' type of fore-knowledge, they also have a great many imaginary fears.

They like careers where they are giving service to others, but can easily sacrifice themselves and live a life of martyrdom. They have high ideals but can be completely unrealistic. Mars in this sign will activate the desire to serve others and good results can be achieved provided they do not fall into the trap of allowing people to dominate them.

Mercury here will make the mind impressionable and there will be a tendency to adopt other people's ideas. The nervous system reacts quickly and as soon as it is put under any sort of strain the Piscean will seek means of escape. Drugs and drink are sometimes used for this, but more often there is a psychosomatic illness of a mental or nervous type. Ulcers are also caused by feelings of being under pressure.

Pisces is associated with the duodenum, pituitary gland, lymphatic system and the feet. Weight is often a problem and this is a contributory cause of mucus in the lungs and glandular disorders.

They can relax easily, but they need rhythmic exercise. Dancing is usually enjoyed by them and this is excellent. They are susceptible to food allergies and need to be sure that food and water are pure, as they react badly to anything even slightly tainted.

Once again, I have had to highlight the weaknesses of the zodiacal types, but they also have their strengths. Mars in each sign will work positively as well as negatively and the same applies to Mercury.

All the planets *can* indicate health difficulties, but need not necessarily do so. Saturn, which is the planet of discipline and responsibility, also represents limitation and this might be limitation of movement, for instance. In another birthchart it might indicate an inferiority complex or even a responsibility which, while limiting in itself, was not unwelcome.

It is clear from all this that people's attitudes contribute largely to health or ill-health. If tension is caused by a situation which seems to be beyond remedy, it is, nevertheless, wise to investigate whether it can be mitigated. Self-help groups are available for many conditions, for instance, to give the parents of a handicapped child a break, while giving the child a holiday.

But there are too many people who complain, as one lady did to me that, "Mother won't let me out of her sight". In this case, 'mother' actually enjoyed visitors and one of them had no difficulty in persuading her to let her daughter go to a dressmaking class once a week, provided one of the friends well known to her stayed in the house until her daughter returned. The difficulty which then arose was to persuade the daughter to go as, "I shall only be worrying in case she is playing you up". In these circumstances, it became obvious that, despite her complaints, the daughter enjoyed the role of martyr and was so much 'into her life-script' of being the self-sacrificer that she felt threatened when it was taken away. The truth is that none of us are as indispensable to others as we think. In this case, it was the daughter who needed therapy to help her to break free from this self-limiting script. I have personally known at least two daughters who had got into this particular role so much that they were completely lost after the death of the mother. They found their freedom to be a frightening thing because they had had no identity except as their mothers' daughters. It took years for one of them to make a life for herself and she reminded me vividly of the woman who had said, "I am nothing".

You can understand from this how frightening it can be to lose the life-script. The loss of identity is a shock, one from which some people never recover. This can be seen often in people who have retired from a career with which they have completely identified, especially if they have had to retire early or been made redundant.

If you ask people, "What do you do?", the majority will reply by telling you their occupation, as if they never did anything else. This is a natural response since we tend to classify people in this way and it is usually the first thing we want to know about them. So it is not surprising that they see themselves as the doctor, the butcher, or whatever.

As I like to know what really makes people tick, I tend to ask instead, "What are your hobbies?" Those who reply that they haven't got any (usually they will say it is because they haven't time) are the ones most likely to be in an occupational life-script. These are the people who most need to develop their inner life further, as that script will eventually fail them and they will have to find another role for the rest of their lives.

Other tensions which can damage health arise from not asking for help or not letting people know how we feel. The reason may be because we are afraid of them, or because we are afraid of our own latent feelings of anger. But anger grows in proportion to the time that it is stored and may then burst out in an uncontrollable explosion, or it may go inward, become unrecognisable as anger (even to ourselves) and manifest as a depressive illness or a nervous breakdown.

Whether we are afraid of others or afraid of ourselves, the way to deal with potentially distressing situations is to 'stay in the Adult' and act *promptly*, before we have time to become too emotionally distressed.

There are times when emotion is fully justified and needs to be expressed. A genuine grievance, a bereavement, or a family tragedy are all examples of cases where it is necessary to express anger, grief and even rage. Unless this is appreciated, severe illness can result, so do not let anyone try to snap you out of such feelings before they have been fully expressed.

Fear is a disabling condition and to take avoiding action against the cause of the fear often reinforces it. As an example, most people are afraid of physical pain and tense against it as soon as it is experienced. This aggravates the pain and sets up a vicious circle, pain causes tension, tension causes pain. If you can deliberately relax even when in pain, this will lessen the impact and it is probably the reason why people who are engrossed in some activity hardly notice it. It has been suggested that married women with an outside job have less illness than women who are at home. The latter may be equally busy but have nothing to prevent them from dwelling on their aches and pains. This also happens with the retired man who has completely identified with his work role.

But fear, in whatever form, can only be overcome by being confronted 'head on'. If you fear it — do it. The rewards are great. The heady sensation one gets in the midst of handling the fear reinforces the life spirit. "Here I am *coping* with this thing I dreaded", is a sublime affirmation. After all, there are only two ways to approach fear, to cringe from it or to beat it.

If you feel that such courage of spirit is not for you, take heart. Others have felt the same and risen to challenges splendidly when the occasion arose, never to go back to their former fearfulness.

We need to observe ourselves and our fears and to ask questions about them. What is the exact nature of the fear? The answer to this can be most revealing. You may find that you think you are just afraid of a row, but that in fact you are afraid of the break-up of a relationship. This puts a new light on the problem — is the relationship worth keeping, or is it one where you will always be afraid to express your feelings (i.e. be yourself)? Then you should ask, "What is the worst that could happen in the situation which I dread?" and finally, "Is it *likely* to happen?" So many of our fears are nebulous that it is only when we confront them in this way that we see them for the shams that they really are. "I have been afraid of shadows", said a young woman in an Encounter group, in a moment of enlightenment.

Of course, some fears are only too well justified and if the answer to, "Is it likely to happen?" is in the affirmative, it is helpful to face the possibility and to take all possible steps to mitigate the situation. Some difficulties in life cannot be resolved; they can only be outgrown, so that they cease to affect progress towards self-fulfilment. My example at the beginning of this chapter will serve as an illustration again. Pearls grow from the irritation in the oyster shell.

6
TALENTS AND DEVELOPING
A CAREER

When an astrologer considers suitable careers for a client, he or she will look at the sun and Ascendant in the chart and take into account any strong features; for instance although the sun may be in Scorpio and the Ascendant in Gemini, the client may have Mars 'strong' in its own sign of Aries or perhaps there may be two or three planets in that sign which emphasise it.

The tenth house, the one at the top of the birth chart, is the house of the career. The zodiac sign in this house will often indicate the type of work which the client chooses, so this must be considered as well.

Referring to Robert's chart (see Appendix 1 on page 153) his tenth house is Libra. This strengthens the sun and Mercury in Taurus, since both signs are ruled by Venus, which gives a great appreciation for art and beauty in all its forms, including music. We said that Libra is also a good agent between an employer and the general public. In this case, Robert would be the 'middle man' between the composer and his or her audience.

Your own birth chart will show the sign on the tenth house and you may be interested to see whether your chosen career agrees with it.

The sixth house is the house of work and service, as well as health, and this can also be relevant to the career. In Robert's chart, the sixth house is Gemini. Robert wants to be a violinist and Gemini rules the hands and arms. That sign is also much concerned with interpretation, communication and adaptability, so you can see that in this particular case the sun sign, sixth-house sign and tenth-house sign are all relevant to his chosen career.

Here is a brief summary of the type of work which is indicated by the zodiacal signs.

Aries. Work requiring energy and initiative such as explorer, pioneer, surgeon, soldier, sportsperson, engineer, psychologist and psychiatrist.

Taurus. Finance, nature and art all appeal to Taureans. Suitable careers are stockbroker, treasurer, banker, accountant, economist, farmer, gardener, florist, nurseryman, architect, builder, musician, artist, art dealer.

Gemini needs to be in the communications business. Careers which will appeal to them are journalist, author, dramatist, news reporter, telephonist, teacher, lecturer, linguist, courier, despatch rider, travel agent, chauffeur, commercial traveller, salesperson.

Cancer. Work connected with looking after people such as caterer, hotelier, nurse, home-economics teacher, child-minder. Also in jobs at sea as fishermen or sailors and work connected with the past as historians or antique dealers.

Leo. All careers that call for leadership, or those which are glamorous and dramatic. They make good goldsmiths and jewellers, professional sportspeople, actor-managers, film actors, producers, impressarios, managing directors, public relations officers and entrepreneurs.

Virgo. Work in communications as teacher, lecturer, or critic; in business as secretary or civil servant, in health as dietician, naturopath, public health officer, in precision work including analyst or statistician and craftsmanship of all types.

Libra. Careers in the beauty and luxury trades appeal to Librans. Work as artists, beauticians, hairdressers, antique dealers, jewellers, will appeal to them; also the 'go-between' careers of diplomat, receptionist, auctioneer, valuer, dealer, solicitor and agents of all kinds.

Scorpio. Work which actively helps others or which deals with public welfare attracts these people. Policemen, or policewomen, detectives, undertakers, research workers, surgeons and psychiatrists, or psychiatric nurses are all possible careers.

Sagittarius. The wide-ranging intellect is used in careers such as teacher, lawyer, priest, philosopher, or writer. Work connected with animals, especially horses, and all forms of sports and exploration are further possibilities.

Capricorn. Practical, routine or organising work which gives opportunities for steady advancement will attract Capricornians. Government officials, politicians, administrators, members of the Armed Forces, teachers, scientists, mathematicians, osteopaths, engineers and builders are all found with this sign prominent in their birthcharts.

Aquarius. Self-employment, or some degree of autonomy attracts these people. They become writers, orators, lecturers, scientists, inventors, or astronauts. They are interested in all the new sciences and often take work in television, broadcasting, astrology and astronomy. They should avoid routine, conventional and restrictive work.

Pisces. Is happy in the caring professions as nurse, doctor, priest, or social worker. All careers connected with the sea are suitable and so are the arts, especially as dancer, poet, actor, or writer.

Of course, these lists are by no means exhaustive, but they give some idea of the direction in which the individual might look for a congenial career.

If you are happy with your daily routine, fine. Not all of us want, or need, a brilliant career in order to achieve self-fulfilment. Years ago, I asked a young man who was training to be a farmer what sort of life he wanted. He replied, "Plenty of hard work and someone to share it with", nothing about owning his own farm one day or getting rich. I introduced him to the very girl for him and they have had the most rewarding and fulfilling life, looking after the animals which they love, and bringing up a family.

But for those whose work is a source of worry, or for those who long to achieve an ambition based on their career, the first step, as always, is to define the difficulties and the goals. Ask a few relevant questions. Why is my present work unsatisfactory? Is it the wrong type of work for me, or does the trouble lie solely with the particular circumstances in this company/firm/factory/office? If there is friction, is it because there is a clash of personalities, or because people have differing goals?

You will easily think of other questions to ask yourself so that you are able to define the problems precisely. By now you should have a good idea of the things you do which cause your own problems. If the fault is yours, or partly yours, arrange to put the matter right. If you discover that your ambitions are always likely to be thwarted in this particular job (perhaps because there are too many people ahead of you, waiting for 'dead-men's shoes' and your employers always promote the most senior members) start looking for a more go-ahead company.

It may be necessary because of the economic climate to retain an unsatisfactory position for some time, but circumstances will change and if you have a clear goal ahead you should keep it in mind. Use the time to get better qualified for your chosen career so that you are ready when opportunities come.

I warned that if you wanted to change that unsatisfactory picture that you saw, only you could do it — and that means work; giving time to analysing yourself, your motives and your circumstances and then working to improve or correct deficiencies. There is a Spanish proverb which runs, "'Take what you want', says God, 'Take it and pay for it'", and it is likely that we can get most of the things we want if we are prepared to pay for them. They cost time, work, attention and all that we are. Only you can know whether your goals are worth the effort. If you decide that some are not, abandon them, but do not continue to brood about them and regret that you did not achieve them.

We have looked quite deeply at the shortcomings likely to manifest with each zodiacal type, so now let us see what each has to offer and learn how to capitalise on our strong points.

How would you like to appear to your employer? And to the general public, if your work brings you into contact with them? Here are some qualities. Choose which are relevant to you: business-like, competent, an achiever, a good organiser, a problem-solver, an ideas person, ambitious, genial, relaxed, serious-minded, reliable, a hard-worker, fair, dynamic, adaptable, kind, protective, helpful, farseeing, responsible, a person of vision, a fighter, humanitarian — enough to be going on with, but by no means exhaustive.

Some of the list may surprise you, but much depends on the type of work. A television interviewer, for instance, would want to appear genial and relaxed to the public if they needed to put someone at ease. To his or her boss they might want to appear as a competent, dynamic, 'ideas' person.

Note the phrase 'want to appear'. It means the same as 'the way we like to project ourselves' and is shown by the Ascendant. So your Ascending sign is likely to be a good indication of the way you appear to other people. The sign on the tenth house may also be relevant as it denotes public status, as well as the career. In many birthcharts that I have analysed, the tenth house sign has described 'the public self' better than the Ascendant so both should be kept in mind.

CAREERS AND THE ZODIAC

Aries. If the Arien is ambitious for a career, he or she will not be satisfied with anything less than the highest position in their chosen field. They perform well under pressure and are likely to be business-like and competent. They will have plenty of ideas and will be more than willing to fight for them. They are likely to be dynamic and aggressive. They will be wasted in work where these talents are not required and should aim to make a change as soon as possible. In the meantime, they could help themselves by learning management skills to enable them to get the best from subordinates and to teach them not to 'ride roughshod' over other people. They have the enthusiasm to motivate, if they can get others on their side.

Taurus. The Taurean is capable of becoming a big business person in a well-established financially sound organisation. Whether they choose this type of career or not, they will always be reliable, responsible and good back-up people. They can increase their chances of success considerably by learning thoroughly all that they can about their chosen subjects. If they limit themselves to a narrow field, they will have the capacity to become experts in it, as they enjoy learning when they can see an end product and they will have a shrewd idea of the value of their expertise.

Gemini. Adaptability is the great forte of the Geminian. They are the people who can turn their hand to anything, in a physical sense, while their mental agility enables them to 'think on their feet'. If politics attracts them, this can be a valuable asset. Being quick-minded, they can be at their best under pressure, or where situations are constantly changing. These are the skills they should be marketing. They need to take training which will build their confidence in themselves so that they can use their qualities of salesmanship to 'sell' themselves and to acquire the discipline to finish one project before starting another.

Cancer. The Cancerian should be able to impress his or her employers with competence and the great skill to look after other people's needs. Cancerians should go into the sort of work where this is important. Practical ability may go to waste unless competence can be 'proved' by paper qualifications and the Cancerian would be well advised to qualify in his or her chosen subject. I put 'proved' into quotation marks because I do not believe that the ability to pass examinations necessarily proves that anyone is competent, except at passing examinations. Alas, in our modern world progress may be halted without them, but luckily there is ample opportunity for anyone to study at whatever age and many people are taking advantage of Open University or other courses, even after retirement.

Leo. Leos should have little difficulty in selling themselves, but may tend to overdo their enthusiasm for their own capabilities, so that potential employers may be suspicious of an 'oversell'. Their great assets are breadth of vision and skill as organisers. They are not afraid of big projects and will work hard. They can inspire others and, if they have not already got them, would benefit from acquiring management skills.

Virgo. Competence, hard work and the capacity to take great care with details are the special skills of the Virgoan. They would provide excellent back-up for an Aries or Leo leader. If they want to assume leadership responsibilities themselves, they must learn how to handle staff, especially learning to appreciate the value of giving praise when it is merited. Reliability and responsibility are worth a great deal to any employer and Virgoans should not underestimate their own worth.

Libra. The Libran may well be a person who is not particularly interested in a career, as long as the working life is pleasant. Their fairmindedness and diplomacy would make them good members of a team, even the leader of it, if such was their aim. However, they are often better self-employed or in a business partnership. Like the Taurean, their sense of value is good. If they want a career, they need to learn how to motivate themselves.

Scorpio. Dedication to a project with the capacity to concentrate well and the resolve to complete it are the special attributes of the Scorpio native. They are good problem-solvers with some orginality of thought. These skills should ensure a good career, but they need to be bolstered with self-confidence and freedom from undue concern with other people's opinions.

Sagittarius. Like their opposite number, Gemini, the Sagittarian's great advantage is adaptability. A variety of interests, plenty of ideas and a relaxed, genial manner make it easy for them to get on with other people, which can be a great advantage in many types of work where meeting people is necessary. They are the people to pull off a big business deal on the golf course, act as Master of Ceremonies at a social event or host a TV talk show. They would benefit from concentrating on one or two

103

subjects relevant to the chosen career and then studying them in depth.

Capricorn. The Capricornian is the one most likely to be ambitious for a career and seems to be born knowing how to achieve it. Their reliability and tenacity usually ensure success, though it may be late arriving. They should recognise that they are not quick thinkers and choose the career accordingly. Like Virgos, they need to learn the value of encouragement to subordinates. One of their most valuable attributes is their attitude to time. They will take the time needed, without waste and without hurry so that their considered opinion is well worth having; it will have been carefully thought out and all possibilities will have been considered. They make good problem-solvers, provided that the solutions do not have to be reached quickly.

Aquarius. A generator of ideas, many of which will be original and inventive, describes the Aquarian at work. To their friendly and humanitarian attitude, they add the power to inspire others and a willingness to fight for worthwhile causes. With such attributes they can reach positions of power and leadership, perhaps as politicians or as a modern crusader. Whatever the chosen field, the Aquarian needs to keep his or her feet on the ground. They can become obsessive or eccentric in the pursuit of ideals, and lose credibility.

Pisces. The Piscean who is a daydreamer may not be motivated towards a career. If they are ambitious for themselves, they are likely to want to be great actors, dancers, poets or writers. They are quite capable of the dedication necessary to achieve their aims, but will need discipline and perseverance which do not come easily to them. They are likely to settle for the job satisfaction of feeling that they have been helpful to others.

By now, you should have recognised your astrological type, or mixture of types and recognise your strengths and weaknesses, so it is appropriate now to look at some general ways of achieving aims and making the most of talents.

The sequence begins with education, not only in a specific subject, but also in developing administrative know-how and professionalism. An American teaching school sets out a philosophy of achieving in the following way.

A. A person learns only from his or her own experience. It is the individual's *participation* which creates learning, not the teacher's role. The individual's own reading, thinking, questioning and writing are important.

B. A leader must know. They must know their subject, but they must also know themselves. Leadership involves influencing others, so a leader must have a knowledge of human behaviour. They understand other people's values, motivations, strengths and weaknesses.

C. A good administrator may not always be a leader, but their administrative skills will be applicable to many fields of operation.

D. Knowledge of yourself includes identifying your personal goals, drives, motives, shortcomings, etc., and whether your commitment as a leader is to a cause, a group or yourself.

E. There is no substitute for work. Worthwhile things come from hard work and careful planning.

F. Welcome challenges. 'When the going gets tough, the tough get going.'

All of this is appropriate, but we have already seen that the big business person is the one whose health may suffer in their drive for success, so we want to operate with ease and confidence. The secret of this is to learn how to 'distance' oneself. While I may be a big business person, I am a great deal more than that. I must not get trapped into this lifescript, so that it becomes the *only* person I am.

Perhaps it would be appropriate at this stage, to write down your present aims. Be aware that they will change as your life proceeds and be prepared to redefine them at intervals.

Let's make it more specific. Take a little time to do this exercise.

Write down the ways in which you want to improve your own

behaviour. For instance, do you need to be more attentive to the problems of others? More willing to consider new ideas? Be less self-conscious when speaking in public? A little slower to criticise and quicker to praise?

Now look at each object you want to achieve in improving your behaviour and consider whether it is a *symptom* of something else. For instance, if you are impatient with other people, it may be because something is bothering you — something inside *you*, perhaps? See what really needs attention, then list the goals you would like to achieve in order of priority. Are they realistic? Will they stretch you? Help you to grow as a person? Do you need the help of others? Do you need resources (money?) to achieve your goal? If so, can you borrow it? Can you be patient until you have earned it? Are you aware of what help is available from government sources, banks, etc.?

Write out your immediate actions. For instance, you might list:

1. Visit Citizens Advice Bureau to see how government help can be obtained.
2. Make appointment with bank manager and discuss a proposition.
3. Sound out a friend who might collaborate.
4. Arrange to attend an evening class.
5. Get literature on Open University.
6. Discuss everything with astrologer/counsellor, etc.
7. Find out what the local library has to offer in the way of books on your subject and information on local courses of study.

I would urge on you the necessity to define your needs and objectives, plan your campaign accordingly and then have the courage to take the step which you fear.

I would also add a few warnings. It is false efficiency to put a lot of effort into the wrong task or the right tasks at the wrong time. You can waste a lot of time and effort if, in the long run, the work does not achieve the intended objective. It follows that you need to be sure what you want to achieve. Time spent on thinking and planning is never wasted.

Effort is often wasted because it is directed to apparent problems, rather than the real ones and symptoms are dealt with instead of causes.

The greatest obstacle to achievement is fear. It can ruin

106

health, sap strength, take away confidence and condemn the individual to a second-rate life. Here is some good news. *It is an impostor*. Face it and it slinks away. Do the thing you fear and you will never fear it again. If it doesn't retreat at once, beat it again. You will get so used to doing the feared thing that you will end up wondering why it ever worried you. Two things which may help you are firstly to ask yourself what is the worst thing that could happen in the circumstances you dread (it is rarely as overwhelming or final as you had thought) and secondly, to recognise that to attempt something and fail is not a disgrace and is no bar to eventual success.

Sometimes circumstances may throw you off course for a while, but it is better to have a course to follow, and to get back to, than to drift with the tide.

I would like to add a few words relevant for the career woman, though some of the situations may apply to men also. Here are some common errors made by women on their way to the top.

1. Failing to let people know your ambitions. You can be thought of as someone who is good as a 'back-up' colleague without ever being considered as a leader, though you could make a good one. There is often an assumption that a *woman* does not *want* a top job. Consider this graffiti seen in a ladies rest room in a top restaurant, 'Women who want equality are unambitious'.

2. Thinking that you need a business partner when you might do better on your own (and vice versa). Consider carefully what qualities the business demands of its managers. Have you got them all — flair for fashion (if it's that sort of business), financial acumen, the drive to go out and find contracts, an ability to get on well with others, salesmanship? If so, consider going it alone, even if it means starting small. If not, find someone who complements your business qualities. In the latter case, make sure that the contract between you is explicit and get it drawn up legally.

3. Complaining about anything you see as discrimination. The way to tackle this one is to tell the management that they are not getting their full value out of you, since your qualifications for better work are indisputable (they'd better be!) and that your professional progress depends upon your getting further experience as soon as possible.

4. Seeing your loyalty to a company (or a boss) as more important than your own career. This is a typically female reaction and one that the management would not necessarily expect from a man, being well aware that the high-flyers change jobs frequently, after learning all they can from that particular one. Women have been known to refuse promotions because they had no intention of staying with a company and felt that it was unfair to the management, thus depriving themselves of valuable experience at a higher level, so that they could start their next job that much further up the ladder.

5. Not valuing extra-mural contacts with colleagues. If the men go for a drink and invite you to join them, think yourself lucky. You'll learn a lot from these sessions, perhaps about the company's future plans, possible vacancies and chances of promotions. Most career women get excluded from the 'old boy network' and get their facts the hard way — often too late. If you are one of these, assume your right to accompany the men and just go and join them.

6. Listening to rumours that affect you personally and then worrying about them. This is a case which calls for confrontation. Say (politely) that you have heard this rumour and ask if there is any truth in it. You can only make decisions if you know the facts.

7. Thinking that the promotion of other women is a threat to your position. The reverse is true, the more women who are promoted into decision-making positions, the better for all women. One day, it will be the best *person* who gets the job. All other things being equal, encourage women to go for promotions and help them if you can.

You know that putting people down can be deliberate, with the intention of 'stroking' yourself, but be on guard against doing it from sheer thoughtlessness. I have just seen a man blow his possible election as chairman of a committee. At the last meeting, having had his offer accepted to host a social get-together, he turned down suggestions of help from most people present, with answers like, "Oh no, we don't want to do that — it's so ordinary". I sat and watched them all decide that they didn't want him in a position of authority over them. Such a pity. He had all the qualifications except tact. So my final word on success in business is this, whatever your work for yourself or for others, learn how to handle relationships.

7
SPIRITUAL GROWTH

As we move forward in this Age of Aquarius we are seeing an upsurge of interest in many forms of spiritual teachings. From the charismatic movement inside the established orthodox churches of the West to the adoption of Eastern religions like Buddhism and Taoism, the spirit of humanity is searching as never before to find a deeper meaning to life.

It has been said that the failure of many of the established religions to provide spiritual inspiration makes it necessary for us to realise that the true source of power is within the human being.

If this is so what can we deduce about spiritual potentiality from the birth chart?

The subject is complex, but it is made even more difficult by the fact that it is also full of paradox and apparent contradictions.

We are all one brotherhood with the same path to tread. In another sense, we are completely on our own and have to work out our own salvation. Also, every spiritual step forward is, in effect, a little death; every insight is a loss, because we cannot hold the vision. We know while it lasts, that *this* is how life really *is* and would always be if it were not for the physical body which intrudes, so life seems a little bleaker when the vision fades. Nevertheless, a gain has been made, for one can never go back to 'un-knowing'.

At every step on this path, there is a need to re-examine our beliefs and our teaching. Consider the phrase 'the best things in life are free'. Money cannot buy health, the beauty of nature, the soul's progress or love, but all can be lost by neglect. What they cost is time, thought and attention as we are beginning to realise with our pollution problems. A lot of soul-searching and suffering is often the cost of the spiritual path.

One teaching advocates that we should be 'in the world but not of it', yet in current psychological parlance we are required to 'be here, now'. I recently met a man who was working a 14-hour day and frequently doing five weeks at a stretch when even his weekends were working days. I asked him how he kept going and his reply was that he had learned how to meditate 24 hours a day.

We tend to think of people who can do this as being shut away in a peaceful retreat but this is not necessary. He had found a way to 'be here, now' and be 'inside himself'.

He was referring to a type of meditation in which one is completely relaxed and yet fully aware and in charge, functioning with full power, but without strain; but 'meditation' is fast becoming a blanket word for many techniques, some of which are not acceptable in our society. Some types are made substitutes for action (or excuse, for non-action) and not infrequently they lead to spiritual pride and concentrate too much attention on the self. Some zodiacal types are already too concerned with themselves and certainly do not benefit from this.

It is not, in my experience anyway, a method of obtaining the 'peak experiences' which the psychologist Abraham Maslow describes — these seem more likely to occur when least expected, as a gift, and not as something for which one has consciously worked. Nevertheless, meditation of the right type can be extremely helpful for some zodiacal-sign natives more than others.

From my point of view, the birthchart is a perfect example of 'being here, now', a blueprint for this one life, and it should be able to indicate the lessons we need to learn at this stage of our long process of soul evolution.

I think it is important to realise that, according to our make-up, whether primarily extrovert or introvert, we all react differently to identical stimuli. Even though we know this, we all assume from time to time, that all reasonable people (meaning those who agree with us) will feel uplifted or repelled by anything to which we ourselves react in that way. This is a fallacy.

In *The Farther Reaches of Human Nature*, Abraham Maslow gives the reason why we should be concerned with the spiritual potentiality of the birthchart. "We must have better human beings, or else it is quite possible that we may all be wiped out — or certainly live in tension and anxiety as a species", and he defines the good person as "the self-evolving, responsible for himself and his own evolution person — the fully illuminated, the fully human". He goes on to say, "It is quite clear that no social reforms, no beautiful constitutions, programmes or laws will be of any consequence, unless people are healthy enough, evolved enough, strong enough and good enough to understand and want to put them into practice in the right way." This seems to me to be a true and most important statement.

I propose now to analyse the zodiac and look at each planet

and sign separately, as if we were only vibrating to one at a time, but it is important to remember that we respond to all the energies of the planets and signs in our birthcharts, whether emphasised or not. The individual has a natural affinity with some of the signs and our job is to extend that affinity until it includes the whole — each new conscious response is an attempt to embrace that wholeness.

The following is an interpretation of the planets as they affect the spiritual life.

SPIRITUAL GROWTH AND THE PLANETS

The **sun** represents the aspiring soul and it is noticeable that most of us grow more like our sun sign as we get older. Its positive characteristics are the ones which we should aim to develop.

The **moon** is very much a 'this life' influence, representing as it does, the gut reactions, childhood experiences and decisions and the feelings which attach to this body in this life.

The nearest planets to the earth all relate to earthly existence.

Mercury, ruling the intellect and communications, can at times be the deceiver and mischief-maker for which his namesake among the gods was noted. I recently met a lady at a conference who told me she was 'off' communications with others because she had begun to despair of finding the right words to make her meaning clear, and once I had a hilarious experience of this when a German friend with a reasonable knowledge of English attempted to board a bus which was full, only to be told by the conductor, "Come on, get off". Her expression of bewilderment was quite something!

The English language is not the only one to perpetuate such confusion. No wonder that Mercury is not much of a spiritual helper in this context.

Although we have been told that the Kingdom of God is within us, many of us act as though the kingdom of the mind were greater and are always seeking outside ourselves for what is in our own souls. Like the children in Maeterlinck's *Blue Bird*, who found that happiness was in their own backyard after all their adventures, so the questing soul sets out to find what it has always possessed.

Venus is in many ways the most material of the planets, ruling material possessions as well as the type of affection which is nothing if not reciprocated, by which I mean that the affection embraces those near and dear to us and is not extended to all indiscriminately. Venus does not represent spiritual love.

The position of **Mars** in a chart, the motivation and driving force, often indicates what the native is driving at, what is the prime motivation for *this* life. The energy and vitality are earthly. This is not a bad thing. We have to live on this earth however much we may aspire. A weak Mars often makes for great difficulties both physically and spiritually because of the lack of incentive.

Both **Jupiter** and **Saturn** have a duality of purpose. Jupiter's expansion can be materialistic in the extreme, but it can also be the expansion of consciousness, the wider vision. Saturn is a teacher on both levels and has been described as typifying the reincarnating soul descending into matter, so both of these can be considered when studying the spiritual forces at work in the birthchart.

The outer planets, like Saturn, all in their individual ways stir things up and cause manifestations on a material or earth level, which can be turned to spiritual account.

Uranus is called the 'higher octave' of Mercury; it communicates at the 'higher' level of inspiration, a communication in which there is none of Mercury's

112

propensity for causing confusion. Messages received on the Uranian level are crystal-clear.

Uranus moves slowly, and is generally regarded as an influence on generations since it will be in the same zodiacal sign for people born in each period of seven years. Uranus can be considered strong if the sign which it rules, Aquarius, is important in the chart, or if the planet itself is prominent by being near the Ascendant, Midheaven or sun.

Neptune is the planet most often linked with mystics and mystical experiences. Its emotional content connects it with Venus, but at a higher level. Love is freely extended to all, not in a sentimental way, but in recognition of our common humanity. It also has connections with the moon, the feelings being less at the mercy of inhibiting psychological factors and more sensitive to what we may call 'higher' vibrations. I think of Neptune in this connection, in its own element of the sea, rather like a formless sea plant which is waving tentacles in all directions ready to pick up the slightest vibrations which can reach it on the constantly shifting tides. Neptune remains in the same zodiacal sign for about 14 years.

Pluto is the 'refining' planet, continually bringing to consciousness those hidden things which must then be discarded and forgotten if there is to be progress psychologically or spiritually. (Forgetting is important — there must be no dwelling on past difficulties.) Pluto has been described as the higher octave of Mars, but I doubt whether it can be classified in this way, except perhaps for one thing. Mars goes straight into action, as if it knew what to do without having to think about it, sometimes with disastrous consequences. Pluto has the same effect on a higher level. There is a sure inner knowledge of when it is right to make a complete change in a life-style, which owes nothing to commonsense.

I am not at all sure that Pluto is so far away from us that it has only an influence on the generations as the text books tell us even though it spends 21 years in each sign. It seems more likely to me that all the outer planets work in an inner sense and on a spiritual level and because their workings are unseen, the idea that their influence is general has gained credence.

I have been using the phrase 'psychologically and spiritually' because I have found when looking at each sign of the zodiac in turn, that what was right psychologically also seemed to be right spiritually. If, for instance, in order to create wholeness in a psychological sense you need to cultivate a sense of detachment, this is also the way to spiritual progress. The aim is to make the individual a 'whole' person in both senses. My great quarrel with most psychologists has been that they have taken no account of the spiritual side of life — I'm sure that this is why it is a common saying that a good psychiatrist can bring you back from hell into 'normal neurosis' (but no further) and it is most encouraging to see the growth of this realisation of the essential oneness of the psychological and spiritual among some of our more enlightened psychologists, many of whom are also astrologers.

SPIRITUAL GROWTH AND THE ZODIAC

Joan Hodgson's book, *Wisdom in the Stars*, categorises the signs under their triplicities. She says that the lessons which each triplicity needs to learn are: Fire signs, love; Earth signs, service; Air signs, brotherhood; and Water signs, peace. This is a reasonable guide, although all, especially the Earth signs, are more complicated than this. As this represents a useful working hypothesis, the signs are grouped in their own triplicities.

There can be no doubt that she is right about the Fire signs needing to learn love. The love is neither Eros nor Agape, but the love which recognises the worth of every human being. All the Fire signs are self-oriented.

Aries often appears thoroughly selfish, mostly due to thoughtlessness, and lack of consideration for others is common. Their drive and power needs to be used in leadership situations, which often bring out the best in them, making it necessary for them to be considerate of others. In such situations, they are capable of considerable self-sacrifice. John Addey, writing on the nativity of Christ gave an Arien Ascendant and "greater love hath no man, than to lay down his life for his friend." On the other hand, the last thing an Arien type wants to do is to fall into the hands of some psychologists who urge, "Be yourself and do your own thing", with the hidden implication, " and to hell with everybody else's rights." Ariens are prone to do their own thing far too much. The way to spiritual progress for them demands a certain amount of self-sacrifice and a recognition of the worth of others. This could help them to achieve the stability for which they seem always to be seeking — causing them to dart in every direction and leaving them unfulfilled.

The typical **Leo** native is self-expressive. They really do feel they are 'special', which is no bad thing too. We are all special, excitingly individual and full of potential, and it would be a good thing if we *all* realised this, as Leo does. However, as W.S. Gilbert said, "When everyone is somebody, then no-one's anybody" and no-one realises this more than Leo. They are more 'somebody' than anyone else, and their spiritual progress has to be along the path of recognition of the unique quality of others. This is the sort of love which they need to extend, to love others "as themselves". It is all part of the psychological necessity not to take themselves too seriously. Leo was born to be a lover of life which is the gift of the ruler, the sun. It is a disaster if they allow their sense of self-importance and dignity to prevent them from celebrating life to the full.

Sagittarius is self-sufficient; one of the signs which feels free to be itself, and they are often psychologically well-adjusted. They take their freedom for granted and have a relaxed attitude to life. Their wide tolerance for other people often does not mean much. It is easy to be tolerant of those who do not matter to you and this attitude can be both the Sagittarian's strength and weakness.

To cultivate detachment on the spiritual path is something to strive for in the case of many people who find it most difficult to achieve, and only after long years of involvement with others. If it comes easily, it is hollow and nothing has been gained. The Sagittarian needs to remember that "No man is an Island, entire of itself" and, to quote Donne further, "Any man's death diminishes me, for I am involved in Mankind." You will realise that, in each case, I am speaking of the lessons for the unevolved soul. There is no doubt, of course, that the many who enter the caring professions, such as the priesthood, etc., already feel the need to fill this gap.

All the Fire signs need to recognise the worth of others.

I am going straight on to the Air signs now, as positive signs all have in common over-concern with the self, and the negative signs are over-concerned with others.

Joan Hodgson said the Air signs needed to learn brotherhood, so consider them in this light.

Gemini is almost totally taken up with his or her many interests. The Mercurial ruler gives them boundless enthusiasm for the things of the mind, and their duality is of mind and hand, rather than mind and heart. They find it difficult to listen to the inner self, or to be still long enough to do so.

Feeling needs to be cultivated, together with the expression of love in brotherhood. Geminians are often

116

attached to their siblings, the attachment needs to be extended.

I once knew a most remarkable Geminian who was a theosophist, an ordained priest, a homeopathic chemist and a published poet and when I tell you that I met him when I was helping him to run his vegetarian hotel you will realise just how versatile a Geminian he was. One of his poems was called 'Friends', which describes the Gemini type and contains a message for all of them. It began:

> I took to myself a friend and found
> I had embraced not one man, but many men
> We sparkled to each other in scintillating colours
> and I became to him like a many-faceted jewel
> He also, to me

and it ended:

> Friends we are, the many in one, and the one in many
> What is it that divides us save the *strong*
> *Fatal illusion* of separateness. (My italics.)

Libra is the representative of balance. Librans are charming, diplomatic, weigh up both sides, etc., and it is true that they do have a great passion for justice, but many of them, and certainly most Librans as children, are like Mrs Gummidge, in *David Copperfield*, whose constant cry was, "I feel it *more* than other people".

While it is true that Librans are sensitive, the result of their preoccupation with themselves is that they quickly resent anything which is even slightly unfair to them. "It's not fair", is the constant cry of the Libran child and sometimes they go all through life seeming to look for grievances. Their lesson is to learn that life is *not* fair, the nicest people get the hardest knocks.

The Libran's way of learning brotherhood is to realise

117

that others have just as difficult a path through life and that many are much worse off than them. 'Count your blessings' might be a good motto for every Libran.

It is also accepted that Librans are basically gentle people, wanting to lead a quiet and comfortable life. Being oriented towards partnership, they often find a partner with whom they live, if they are lucky, in this comfort and contentment, shutting their eyes, as far as possible, to the troubles of others and living in their own little world. The demand of the spiritual path for Librans is that they go out and offer this feeling for the partner, together with their sense of justice, to others, which, of course, a great many evolved souls already do.

Turning now to **Aquarius**, you may think that the Aquarian has already learned the lesson of brotherhood; their humanitarian side is so well-known. But what is the other thing for which this type is noted? Passion for personal freedom, which they feel is always threatened so that they must be ever wary to defend it. The dilemma of the Aquarian is the dilemma of the Aquarian Age, they want fair shares for all and absolute freedom for everyone, which does not work in practice for there must be rules to give everyone fair shares and rules threaten freedom. This dilemma can only be resolved when the children of Aquarius are prepared to give up a little of their precious freedom in the interests of all.

In personal relationships, Aquarians feel that to reveal themselves threatens their freedom. Even in close ties they feel the net closing in. One typical Aquarian response to learning that I was an astrologer was a shudder, with the comment, "I would hate to have anyone suss me out".

But lasting relationships can only be made at a deep level of understanding and this can only be done by being willing to reveal oneself: to draw back from this is, in effect, to draw back from life.

We now come to the negative signs, all of which tend to be over-concerned with others, though the Earth and Water signs do this in totally different ways.

The Earth signs are largely compulsive and obsessive types, and although they do give service to others, it often seems to be in a judgemental, discriminating fashion. They are practical people who need to see results.

Where the Fire signs need to see the uniqueness of each individual, the Earth signs need to appreciate their common humanity.

Taurus has the reputation for possessiveness and for being over-interested in possessions and certainly I have met several who were downright mean, not only with possessions, but in their desire to get the most for themselves. They have a psychological need to be 'earthed' to give them a feeling of stability and security. (It took me years — I have a Taurean moon — to learn that security was a myth). Taureans have to learn to give away in order to gain. In the words of the poem, to purchase "hyacinths to feed the soul", or, to quote Tolkien, "He who cannot part with a treasure at need is in fetters".

The sign of the Bull has ancient connections with the worship of Mithras, the slayer of the Sacred Bull, who "went consenting" to the sacrifice. Many things come to us in life which we would rather not have, but I have never believed that astrology (or indeed, anything or anyone) *makes* us react in particular ways. How we meet our difficulties is up to us and it seems to be demanded of Taureans, more so, perhaps than any of the Earth signs, that they should make willing sacrifices — and it certainly is a sacrifice to them to share freely with others. Sharing is also, as many Taureans find, its own reward.

Virgo is noted for a strongly critical attitude, which they apply equally to themselves as to others, often

119

setting themselves impossibly high standards so that they are forever doomed to failure. They are hedged about with 'oughts and shoulds' ('I should' and 'he ought' are typical Virgoan phrases) and the service which they give to others is tempered by criticism and is sometimes withheld from those who they consider are not worthy.

They need to come to terms with their own humanity and that of others and learn to love it. We can only give real service if we understand others and are ready to accept them 'warts and all' and not expect too much of them, or of ourselves, since we are all fallible human beings. The Virgoan is one who would benefit from the type of meditation which enables them to discover, appreciate and truly become what they really are.

There is a great deal more in all of us than is represented by any one sign of the zodiac and we could all benefit by learning to celebrate both our common humanity and our individuality, the ways in which we are unique and the ways in which we are all alike, thus truly becoming 'whole'.

This applies particularly to the native of **Capricorn**, the Saturnine, responsible and patient character, who sometimes controls feelings to freezing point and becomes tense and restricted as a result. They share with Cancer the distinction of being one of the worriers of the zodiac. All the same, their service to others is practical and they can be a very present help in times of trouble, as many people have found to their advantage. Their rock-like qualities make them reliable friends, but, like Aquarians, they find it difficult to reveal themselves — in their case, because they really don't *want* to know themselves. There might be a genie in a bottle waiting to be released, who knows with what results. Like the Virgoan, they need to learn the whole content of their unique selves and to accept themselves and others in all their many facets, and not be judgemental. Their ambitions are not for glory, but for power and these positions can be lonely and need to be handled wisely if the power is not to corrupt. A dedication to the service of others is one way to make sure that it does not.

When we come to the Water signs, we come to a totally different kettle of fish. These people are all emotion, aware of their common humanity, but much less aware of their uniqueness. Until now we have been talking about people who need to learn to relate to others. Although I said quite truly that the Earth signs are overconcerned with others, it is in a judgemental way and they do need to learn to get closer to people. The Water signs are far too concerned with others already and I think Joan Hodgson is quite right in saying they need to find peace and this means detachment from others, for we can only find true peace inside ourselves.

Cancer is the archetypal mother sign. Tenacious like the crab, they find difficulty in letting their grown-up children go. Like Taureans they need to remember to 'hold close with open hands'. Most of their worries are for family or friends and the mother type must realise that no matter how much she loves them, she cannot carry *their* burdens, but only her own. *Their* difficulties, *their* path of progress, belong to them. Cancerians need to learn to be more concerned with their own affairs, their own uniqueness and also to realise that all the worrying they do is not going to detract from other people's difficulties by one iota.

It is true for all the Water types (as well, of course, for everyone) that in the last resort we are all on our own, we have to make our own path, work out our own salvation and no matter how much you love others you cannot do it for them.

I would like to say to all the worriers of the zodiac (and I come from a long line of them) that it is possible to train yourself not to worry, but I also know that it is

121

not easy. You have to continually catch yourself at it, as it were, and then resolutely turn your mind to something else. I think it helps to realise that all worrying is a rehearsal for something. We are continually rehearsing how we are going to meet a situation and dwelling on it, over and over again. It may never happen, but whether it does or not, our continual previous dwelling on it will not affect the situation, so all our worry is wasted. Some people seem to regard it as an insurance policy, "If I worry about it hard enough, it won't happen", like a propitiation to the gods. The ancient superstitions lie deep within us all. You remember Shakespeare's *Julius Caesar*, "Cowards die many times before their deaths — the valiant never taste of death but once", so the motto for Cancer is 'Don't worry, it may never happen'. They need to learn how to achieve their own inner peace and this means they have got to be more concerned with themselves and less with others.

Many of the Water types are in the caring professions and anyone who has done any sort of social service knows how often the results are disappointing. The situation often means that a good result is unlikely. If we have done our best, we must be content to leave the results in Higher Hands and allow ourselves peace of mind. More often than not, it is the detached person who is of the greater value in these situations anyway.

The **Scorpio** types have to battle with their own intensity, and they tend to project their difficulties on to other people. They are strongly emotional and passionate. Horatio Nelson was described in a poem as having 'a soul like a North Sea storm'. I discovered recently that he had a Scorpio Ascendant and that phrase has always described Scorpio for me. Scorpios are passionate for life and they need to find the peace at the eye of the storm. They cannot go into retreats to find it. They must be 'involved in mankind'.

They do have the bonus of the rulership of Pluto. When they can listen to their inner promptings they are able to make the necessary changes both psychological and spiritual in their lives and discard completely a whole way of life or a whole psychological difficulty, which has been holding them back. But they won't do it if they are continually worrying about what other people will think. It is this that stops them more often than not from getting to grips with their situation. They know what needs to be done, but the overconcern with other people's reactions or criticisms prevents them. Often, this becomes an inner tension which builds up until the result is explosive — a sudden shattering of a relationship which, perhaps, need not have happened if the situation had been recognised in the beginning. All the secret drives of Scorpio are only secret because they feel other people would not understand them. Their astrological house is the house of death and this has to be from the death of the lower self to a resurrection as a whole person, unconcerned with the opinions of others so long as they know where they are going. I quote from Goethe for Scorpio,

> He who has not got this
> This death and becoming
> Is but a dull guest in a dark world.

The inner search and the sense of detachment are what bring peace at length to the questing soul of Scorpio.

Pisces is adaptable and friendly but at the mercy of the tide and often apprehensive of what it brings to them from others. Rather like Librans, they like a pleasant life and, like their sign, the fish, they will glide out of trouble whenever possible. The tendency to live in a dream world and not come to grips with reality, might also suggest a lack of courage. Nevertheless, W.S. Landor was probably nearer to describing the Piscean's philosophy, "I strove with none, for none was worth my strife". They are strongly intuitive and they need to find peace within and also to appreciate themselves because, with the Virgoan, they tend to underrate themselves. For them also the answer is 'going inward' to experience *themselves* and to learn not to be overconcerned with others, either trying to carry their burdens like Cancer, or fearing their criticism like Scorpio — and Pisces can do both. There is no doubt that Joan Hodgson was quite accurate when she suggested that all the Water signs need to learn how to achieve peace.

Unless we have a commitment to strive for the best that is in us we shall not truly achieve individuation. No-one who is seeking for self-fulfilment will want to leave the world worse off for their life. Indeed, most of us have a strong urge to perpetuate something of ourselves that is worthwhile. We cannot take our possessions or attainments with us, but what we *are* remains and may influence generations to come.

· "Never underestimate the example of a happy marriage", a priest said to my husband and myself. I would say, "Never underestimate the example of a fulfilled life". If you are in a position to help or advise other people, you may be sure that what you are is more important than what you say.

This chapter has urged an awareness of your common humanity with others. This is important for an appreciation that we all have similar hopes and fears, difficulties and triumphs, but what you have to give to others is the unique person that is your true self.

Therefore, far from being afraid of being different from other people, we should welcome the personal contribution that we have to make. I have said already that it is not by chance that we are all different. Why, then, do so many of us feel that there is something wrong with us, if we do not conform to a pattern?

I treasure a comment made by my father as a small boy. A teacher had said to him, "Other boys don't act like that." Telling his mother, the child said, "But I'm not 'other boys', am I?" As little children, we all have a sense of the power of the individual.

If you think that power means wealth and positions of authority, consider some of the people who have made their names and work live because their power was inherent in their capacity to be themselves. Socrates, a poor stonemason with a gift for asking relevant questions; Gandhi, who changed history without the use of force; Martin Luther King; Jesus. The list is endless.

True self-fulfilment is far from being selfish. Rather it enables us to show others how they, too, may become authentic. "To thine own self be true", said Shakespeare, " . . . thou canst not then be false to any man". It sounds good, but is it true? Why can you not be false to anyone else? First of all because you are not afraid to tell them how you see the situation. Lies and subterfuge become unnecessary. They may disagree with you and you may even discover that their view is the correct one. Even if some distress is caused, it will be better to know the truth than to dread it, for once it is known it can be dealt with appropriately.

"Level with me", said a friend to a doctor, "I've got TB, haven't I?" "Nothing of the sort", the doctor replied, "You worry about your health too much. Forget it and take more exercise." The situation was that although my friend asked the doctor to 'level' with her, she should have asked the question months before, when she first started worrying.

I have not yet met a person who did not appreciate another who was authentic enough to tell the truth. In such encounters, it came as a great relief for them to feel that they could respond equally frankly. This is especially noticeable in dealing with deep feelings or spiritual matters. Once they are broached, it is common to discover that these are the subjects people really want to discuss, though most people are far too inhibited to raise such matters themselves in ordinary conversation.

It is fortunate for me that my discipline is astrology because it is a subject of great interest to many people and in the course of explaining the true nature of astrology I find that this frequently leads to a discussion on spiritual values. More often than not the matter is seized on eagerly by a client who is questing for some meaning to life.

This brings me to the reason why I believe that the progress towards spiritual fulfilment is so necessary to the health of the individual. I quote from my book *Astrology and Health*.

> . . . there is no bodily health without spiritual health. By this I do not mean to imply that we should have reached a certain standard of 'goodness' but that we should be aware

of being on a spiritual path — a journey towards a goal. If we are not conscious of this we shall lose our way and our physical health will be affected by a false sense of the futility of life. What is it all about? Is anything worth doing? These are questions we all ask at some stage in our lives. If ... unfortunate events occur, such as we experience occasionally ... we go into what is called 'a nervous breakdown' but which is really a spiritual crisis. ...

Various psychological therapies ... are valuable tools. We outgrow old beliefs, but fail to update them, and we all know those who need to come out from the shadow of others and find their own self-esteem ... but the ego-centred existence carries its own dangers, and ... if followed to the extreme, cuts us off from other human contact.

The way of spiritual progress differs for all of us, but this matters little. Allegiance to the Masters, whether Jesus, Buddha, Mohammed, Confucius or any other messenger, should mean a recognition that the message is more important than the speaker. All these teachers taught us that and many of them conveyed much the same message, though adapted for the people to whom they spoke. All recognised the value of the individual.

There are two pictures of spiritual life which I would like to share with you. The first is of a great diamond which represents all truth. It fell to earth and was shattered into fragments. The people seized the bright little jewels and took them home, rejoicing for each said to themselves, "Now I alone possess the truth".

The second scene is of a great mountain. Pilgrims of all faiths are ranged around its base, each group far apart from the others. Each thinks that they are on the only path which will lead to the summit. Everywhere they follow winding roads, some of which peter out or lead them back to their starting point. But from every group some begin to climb and slowly the different ways converge. At last, on the summit, all paths are one.

8
PROGRAMMED FOR SUCCESS

We never make New Year resolutions in my home, but around that time of year one of us will ask, "Are your options still open?" The answer is still a resounding "Yes", even though my husband and I are considered 'Senior Citizens'. Life still holds challenges, opportunities and surprises if our eyes are not closed to them and we are prepared to consider anything that comes along.

This does not mean that we are always restlessly looking for change. Life can be fulfilling wherever you are, if you are in charge of it.

Solon is often quoted as saying, "Call no man happy until he is dead" and this has been interpreted as "No-one alive is happy". But the story which he told to illustrate his point makes it clear that his meaning was, until you come to the very end of your life, you cannot judge it, and this is true, for all through life there is the possibility of change if one is willing to recognise it.

Decisions are not irrevocable; situations are often capable of mitigation (as in the case of the lady who thought that she could not leave her mother alone) and opportunities open new doors all through our lives if our minds are not closed to the possibilities.

We are urged towards change by the fact of becoming older, and we need to be aware that there will be no growth unless we are prepared to take risks. How sad to come to the end of a life which has been restricted by fear of change, for life is the great adventure. We are all on a journey and every journey goes into the unknown and contains within it the seeds of fear. We have to learn not to be afraid of being afraid and not to let that stop us.

This chapter considers how to programme ourselves for success and how astrology can help us.

Most people think of astrology as a purely predictive science because of the 'forecasts' given in newspapers and magazines. This is using only one facet of a discipline at its lowest common denominator and most professional astrologers would reject it. However, we all use predictive techniques in our work, based on the movement of the planets now and in the immediate future in relation to the birth chart.

One of the pieces of information which an astrologer uses to interpret a birthchart concerns the aspect, or angle, which two planets make to each other. Depending on the measurement of the angle between them, the facets of the personality which the two planets represent may combine easily or stressfully. Let us imagine that there is a stressful aspect between Mercury (the mind and nervous system) and Mars (vitality and initiative). This may result in nervous strain, overwork or much criticism of other people. At quite frequent intervals, this aspect will be 'touched off', rather like lighting a firework, when the current position of Mars at these times is the same as it was in the natal chart, at the time of birth. Each time this happens the result is identical. The native rushes into action, overworks and blames other people for everything that goes wrong. Yet at the time that the aspect is activated, he or she is, in fact, being given a chance to deal with a problem. The individual can choose *not to react* in their usual way. Once the pattern has been broken, it becomes easier to do so again and eventually the individual will learn that they can choose to *act*, rather than *react*.

But the fact that a particular aspect (planetary relationship) in the chart remains constant means that the individual has to accept a basic temperament which will tend to induce this nervous reaction. He or she cannot prevent it but only learn how to deal with it.

"What can't be cured must be endured", runs the old saw, but endurance implies suffering. Consider, instead, *accepting* instead of enduring.

Acceptance suggests consent, willing reception, recognition that a situation exists which cannot be changed. There is therefore no point in fighting it; much better to be relaxed about it. There is a sense in which such problems which are accepted become outgrown. They cease to affect the quality of life. This is exemplified by the man to whom this book is dedicated.

Of course there are many situations, other than those inherent in one's own character, which are of this nature. Paradoxically, it is often the most distressing and intractable ones which are accepted most readily. The parents of a handicapped child, after the first shock has worn off, may accept the situation philosophically, taking up their burden with the minimum of distress and finding mitigating factors and compensations.

If we want to programme ourselves for success, it will be helpful to consider, not only what we can do, but also what we cannot do, or cannot change. We need to be quite clear that the situation, whatever it may be, can *not* be resolved, either by ourselves or by someone else to whom we could appeal. If such is the case, then we need to accept it and not fight it. More energy is wasted in fighting or regretting situations which cannot be changed than is used productively.

Even in such situations, it is sometimes possible to try a different method of dealing with them which may help to take some of the burden from them. Some apparently irreconcilable problems only need a new approach to solve them completely.

The person with the closed mind will often say, "I've *always* done it that way", or, "In this firm, we *always* do so-and-so". The longer this attitude has persisted, the more need there is to look at new ideas. If you cannot come up with some yourself, never be afraid that asking for ideas from other people will weaken your position. The mature person has enough sense to know that no-one is good at everything and has enough assurance of his or her own worth not to feel at all put down by approaching a colleague or friend for help. If you adopt someone else's idea and give them full credit for it, you will find that they regard you as a wise and sensible person — you must be, otherwise you would not have recognised their worth!

Do not close your mind to any ideas or any subjects by dismissing them as 'cranky' until you have explored them. I have a favourite quotation from Herbert Spencer, who said, "There is a principle which is a bar against all information, which is a proof against all arguments, which cannot fail to keep a man in ever-lasting ignorance; that principle is contempt, prior to investigation." While we need to avoid being gullible, we also need to avoid condemning out of hand. There are far too many things in evidence in this generation which previous ones would have laughed to scorn if they had been predicted then.

I suggest that you do not waste your time on trying to convince people who have this closed mind. If they are not willing to open it, you may knock forever without gaining admission.

In any situation which you want to improve or resolve, the basic approach is always along the lines of careful examination. Ask yourself these questions:

What is my problem or situation? Is there an underlying problem?
How does it make me feel? And act?

129

What does it mean to me?
What can I do about it?
Will I do it? Have I the will to do it? Is it worth the effort?
How will I achieve it?

Do not attempt to attain perfection. Set your own specific upper and lower limits. Sometimes it is true that 'anything worth doing, is worth doing badly'. I have no talent for painting, but I enjoy it as a relaxation, to me it is 'worth doing badly' but it would not be worth my energy to learn to do it well. I would rather save that for things which are more important to me and for which I have some talent.

If you know what your upper and lower limits are, do not let other people pressure you into accepting their standards. Remember, "I am not here to live up to your expectations".

From time to time, it is helpful to sit down and consider your aims and your potential. These will change as years go by and as you achieve some of your ambitions. When you do this examination ask yourself:

What do I really want to do (be, achieve) at this time?
What, if anything, is stopping me?
What do I need, or need to do, in order to be able to do it?

In assessing our own potential, we should be aware that all of us have both a masculine and feminine side to our natures and both need to be expressed. For the masculine side to survive we need to initiate, to have a purpose. This is the authority figure. For the feminine principle, we must express our creativity and the non-rational. The masculine side of us asks, "Where am I going?" while the feminine asks, "Who am I?". Both questions must be answered, if self-fulfilment is to be achieved.

With this in mind, examine your assets.

What is your body's greatest asset (strength, vitality, ease of relaxation, beauty, dexterity, good voice, etc.)? Can you exploit this asset?

Where is your body most vulnerable? Can anything be done about it? If not, accept it, note the situation and leave it. Do not dwell on it.

Is there anything specific which you could do *now* for your body. This should be updated at intervals, so that you can take further steps.

130

In this connection, there was an article in a recent magazine directed at retired people. The writer, a man in his late sixties, resolved to start walking. He did a little every day, gradually increasing his distance. Then he began to run for a little while between the periods of walking. Again he increased this until he spent as much time running as walking. Very gradually he added exercises. He was in church one morning when a strapping young woman in the next pew fainted. Without hesitation, while younger and bigger men were wondering how to get her out of the pew, he lifted her and carried her outside. It seems that he was just as amazed as the onlookers. He had not realised how strong he had become. His doctor confirmed that he had the blood pressure of a young man. Slowly and steadily, the body can be improved at any age.

Now examine your emotions. What is your greatest asset here? Are you tolerant, kind, helpful, a good listener? Where are you most vulnerable, emotionally? Can anything be done about this? Almost certainly, the answer here is that something can be done. I have suggested a book which will give you all kinds of ideas to try (*Games People Play*, see appendix). I would add one warning — many therapies work, *but only as hard as you do*. It is no good being aware that they are available and feeling interested if you do not go on to study them, decide which one is for you and then practise it.

You should ask the same questions about your mind. What is its greatest asset? Is it quick, thorough, intuitive, good at problem solving? How can you exploit these assets? Now decide where your mind is most vulnerable and whether anything can be done about it. If not, accept it and do not waste time on regrets, but be very sure that nothing can be done. Many forms of training are available to improve mental skills. Finally ask yourself if there is anything you can do for your mind *now*.

Success is an attitude of mind. Believe that you can succeed and you will. Do not fall into the trap of 'Try hard' with the hooker of 'don't succeed'. Don't try it — do it.

Believe that you can look after yourself. So many people with problems consider themselves victims, at the mercy of a persecutor, whether 'fate' or just 'they' and are looking for a rescuer. But they do not need one. They are quite capable of dealing with their own problems. Often they are waiting for someone else, or circumstances, to change. They may wait for ever. Such people will be aware of what they dislike about their position, but not aware of what is making them put up with it. This is usually to do with life script. Be aware that you do not need a life script.

Emphasise your personal power and responsibility. Refuse to be put down or discounted by anyone. If you feel overawed by anyone, it is because you have conceived them as a superior to yourself. You can cut them down to size (the size of an ordinary human being) by imagining them in ordinary situations. For instance, the man who bullies his typist is often the victim of an overbearing wife. See him as a henpecked husband and you will never fear his superiority again.

In order to be fully autonomous you need freedom to act, openness to experience and ability to think your problems through to a conclusion. None of these are difficult to achieve.

Decisions need to be made by the whole personality. One which makes sense on a mental level, but does not feel right will cause regrets later. 'If in doubt, do nothing' is often a good adage, provided it is not used as an excuse to duck responsibilities and that a decision can be delayed without worsening the position. If you allow other people to make a decision for you, you must realise that you are opting-out of the situation and are putting them in a position where you can blame them if things go wrong. This is not fair to them and reinforces your own life script of dependence on others. For the same reasons, refuse to make decisions for other people which they should make for themselves. It has been said that, "When we ask advice we are usually looking for an accomplice" (Marquis de la Grange).

Therapists, who have worked with young unmarried mothers who have allowed their babies to be adopted, report that the greatest psychological difficulties arise later if someone else has really made that decision. The parents of a young girl may feel and may persuade her that adoption is the most sensible solution. Her mind may agree with them, but if her emotions tell her otherwise a period of acute depression, guilt and even suicidal tendencies may manifest and take many years to resolve.

Emotions are valid when they are immediate and are an important part of us (the best part, some would argue). Do not be ashamed of your emotions for you share them with every other human being. It is healthy to communicate them. Justifiable anger, love and grief all need to be expressed if we are not to become psychological cripples. No emotions should make us feel guilty, unless we misuse them. For example, we might refrain from expressing justified anger only to punish the other person in

132

some covert way which does not give them the opportunity to come to an understanding, so that the cause of the anger can be removed.

We need to realise that we play these games with other people when we feel vulnerable and therefore we can assume that they do the same thing. So it is helpful to learn as much as possible about others. Spend a little time learning to 'read' people. The study of astrology is one method; another is to learn to interpret body movements. There are many books about this, but much of it is obvious. A lover is not deceived by a verbal assurance of love if he is being pushed away at the same time. A person who sits with her arms folded around herself is not intending to let anyone else come close. If you are talking to an acquaintance and his eyes shift away from you, you have lost his interest.

So ask yourself, what are the body movements saying? What about the pitch of the voice and rate of speech? Sometimes people's clothes reveal a great deal about them. If they often wear bright colours and suddenly appear in sombre ones it is not difficult to guess that they are feeling dejected.

I was once in an office where one of the senior managers was a red-haired man who tended to be abrupt and who was not much liked. Eventually he became my immediate boss and I found him to be a compassionate person with a real interest in his staff. I soon discovered that his abruptness lasted approximately 8.30 to 10.30 a.m. and that he was quite amenable when he had had his coffee and woken up properly. I had to report to him early, but I learned to confine my remarks to, "Good morning. Everyone is in" (or possibly, "So-and-so hasn't reported in yet") and then wait until he sent for me. He turned out to be one of the best managers for whom I have ever worked. I told my staff not to approach him until after the coffee break, with the result that he soon became popular, much to his own surprise. An understanding of another person, even at this superficial level can be worth a great deal in both business and personal relationships.

The subject of timing is an important one. We should all know better than to ask the boss for a favour when he is clearly in a bad mood, but even then it is possible to be so concerned with your own affairs that you do not appreciate how the other person is feeling. If you are to succeed, timing must be right.

Astrology can help here in illuminating the most favourable times for new projects. For many reasons, it is seldom possible for the technique to be used for really accurate forecasts, to the exact hour for instance (though it has happened), but trends can be predicted and will show up clearly when the whole birthchart is studied in connection with the planetary movements prevailing at the time under consideration.

I have already mentioned the possible effect of the moon's cycle on those who have the sign of Cancer emphasised in their charts, but all of us have a natural body rhythm and, if you keep records, you will probably be able to predict your own maximum periods of energy and wellbeing with some accuracy. You may find books on Biorhythms helpful. If you can also apply your findings to others with whom you are in close contact, you will obviously choose the right times for them, as well as for yourself, to start new joint ventures.

Depending on the situation, you may also need to consider whether the time is right economically, emotionally — for instance, if you are not in a stable emotional state following a bereavement, you should not be making major decisions — and practically. As regards practicality, a move to a different town might be good for you, but mean a change of school for your children at a critical time in their education.

I would like to say a word here about the effect of the movements of Saturn on the birth chart. It remains for quite long periods in roughly the same place and during the time when it is affecting certain points on your own birthchart you may experience frustrations and delays. An astrologer would be able to tell you how long these are likely to last. Please do not get upset by such delays, but accept that the time is not right. When something for which you have longed is meant to be, everything slots into place with miraculous ease. Most of us have experienced the dissolution of what seemed to be an insoluble problem, often in ways we could not have imagined. 'What's for you won't go past you' is a favourite family maxim and I remember also that good luck has been defined as being in the right place at the right time *with the right qualifications*. You may not be able to govern the time or the place, but you can make sure that you are prepared to take full advantage of whatever opportunities arise.

Before we leave the subject of 'reading' the body, don't forget to read your own. Feelings of anxiety and all other emotions are expressed through the body. Change the body position and you assume control over the feelings. Relax, breathe deeply, loosen those tight muscles, unclench your fists and the real you is once more in charge and no longer at the mercy of your feelings.

This chapter has had a lot to say about success, but what if you do fail in achieving one of your goals? Should you try again? Much depends on the type of failure. A fault in yourself may be eradicated by practice, but if you failed for a reason outside your control, you need to examine the circumstances. Should you decide to try again, is the possibility of success more likely? You may need to wait until some things — the economic climate, your own financial position, your partner's circumstances — have changed; or you may have to face the fact that success is unlikely in the foreseeable future and put the matter behind you. In any event, do not blame yourself for failure. It is permissible to fail, just as it is permissible to take your time, to plan, to relax and to have (and express) feelings. Don't let other people stampede you into hurrying, continually working, or discounting your own emotions. People do not own people.

Life is meant to be lived and its richness should not depend on other people, although it is likely to include them. Recognise that you have plenty of options and your life will be fulfilled.

9
HELPING OTHERS

Once you feel that you are in charge of your own life, the time is bound to come when you want to help other people to achieve the same state. Although we are not likely to become completely individuated in a life-time, every step of self-development enlarges our horizons and we want to share our experience.

You may have no wish to help the world at large, but you will want your children to be free of life scripts and to help your partner relate to the new you. Perhaps you may be the sort of person to whom friends naturally turn for advice. So this chapter will consider ways of helping others to achieve their own self-fulfilment.

There are several pitfalls to be avoided and no-one should attempt to do counselling for members of the general public (some of whom may be very distressed) without proper training. But you should be able to help others to break away from confining conditions provided you are well aware of the dangers.

First of all, you must know your own psychological hang-ups. It is not unknown for an astrologer with a strong bias to see the same thing in every chart he or she studies and this can be true of all types of counsellors.

The insight which astrology gives into your own character can enable you to appreciate your normal approach. For instance, if you are predominantly a Fire type, who has plenty of energy and is always busy, you may not realise that you are expecting the same high energy level from other people. If you make suggestions for activities to others and they do not respond enthusiastically, it will do no good for you to lose patience with them if the fault lies in their lack of energy. Similarly, a predominantly Earth personality may suffer from a rigidity of mind in the approach to someone else's problems which may prevent the consideration of viable alternatives to the methods which have helped them personally.

What I am saying, of course, is that you need to know yourself well in order to be able to help others. Over the last few years, psychological help has become available in the form of various types of group therapy, Encounter, Gestalt, Transactional Analysis, Humanistic and Transpersonal Psychologies, and others. Attendance at a few seminars or weekend workshops, especially those particularly aimed at people in the caring professions, will soon give you an insight into the types of problems which people have and the right approach to them. At the same time, you will come to understand yourself better and may become aware of some attitudes which you may not have realised you possessed.

You will need to try several groups to discover which suits you best. Not all will meet your needs and you may find some distasteful, so do not be pressured into committing yourself to a full course unless *you* are satisfied that it will be beneficial. Reading some of the recommended books may help you to decide where to begin.

I should make it clear that I am not suggesting that you should act as an unqualified psychologist, even after you have had some training. Indeed, I can think of nothing more dangerous, both for you and your victim, but one of the advantages of having some knowledge of what is available is that you can pass it on to people who need more help than you can give. Sometimes it happens that the person who needs help is too close to you for either of you to be detached enough to benefit from working together. In such a case, you may be able to persuade them to attend some group therapy sessions, but do make it clear that you have done it yourself so that they do not think that you are suggesting that they 'need a psychologist'. Most of us do, but the layperson invariably thinks that he or she is being classed as a nut case or, at least, that they are being regarded as psychologically disturbed.

One thing which often occurs at the beginning of therapy sessions is that each participant is asked, "What are your expectations of this workshop?", or, "What do you hope to get from it?" At later sessions, they may be asked, "What do you want to work on this week?" This approach establishes the fact that counselling is a two-way thing. No-one is imposing a solution or giving instructions. Both the counsellor and the client should be working together as a team. In helping friends, you need to be able to indicate to them what the possible courses of action are as you see them, but always leave them to decide.

Some people will want you to make their decisions for them to avoid responsibility and, perhaps, to have someone to blame if things go wrong. This must be resisted at all costs and such suggestions should be countered with statements like, "It is your life and no-one else can decide for you how you should live it." It is also helpful to ask, "What do you *really* want to do?"

Most of the time it would be appropriate for you to be sympathetic, but occasionally you will meet people with whom it is not wise to use a gentle method and here a bit of shock treatment may work better. Such people are the self-satisfied or the complainers — often they are both. There is a true story here which illustrates the point.

A lady had been visiting patients at a mental hospital and she realised how difficult it was for them to go straight back into normal life once they were discharged. She decided to open a half-way house for them where they could go out to work, but return in the evenings to people who understood their difficulties and to friends who had had the same experiences as themselves. A man came to her for admission and at once began to complain about how thoroughly incompetent everyone had been in handling his case. At the end of his long tirade, he asked her, "And what are you going to do for me?" She replied, "Nothing. I am not going to accept you." "Why not?" he asked in amazement. Her devastating answer was, "I don't want to become another excuse for your failures." However, the story has a happy ending. This nasty jolt was the beginning of rehabilitation for him. He pleaded with her to accept him and she did, first making it a condition that if he ever criticised her or the way the house was run, he would be turned out.

Harsh as it seems, I believe this is the only way that you can deal with people who are always complaining about the way life, or other people, has treated them. They indicate clearly that they are sitting back and letting things happen to them and that *they* are never to blame. These are the ones to whom I use blunt words. "This is your life pattern; this is how you are; this is what you can be if you choose."

In our attempts to help others, nothing is so valuable as experience. If you can say, "I have experienced this myself and I learned to cope with it like this", it is a great help to people who feel that they are completely alone with their problem. If they are distressed, they find it difficult to believe that anyone else has ever been in that position before. But there are few of us who go through life without getting to the stage where we feel in the depths of despair and have to pull ourselves up by our boot straps. Our strength then is to be able to say to another person,

"I have been where you are and I know how you feel."

A friend, who had had major heart surgery involving a valve replacement, having recovered completely, offered his services to the British Heart Foundation. His work was to visit people who were to have the same operation, to reassure them. "You don't have to say much", he told me, "the fact that you've been through it and you're *there* does the job for you." We all draw our strength from the examples of people who have 'been through it', whatever 'it' is because they are the living proof that we can survive our troubles.

If you are helping many people, you will find that all their difficulties are much the same and soon, if you cannot say, "I have experienced it", you will be able to say, "I know someone who had this trouble and this is how they dealt with it." We need to set our own upper limits as to what we can cope with. People who need more help than we can give should be referred to those who are qualified.

But we also need to set lower limits. Do not let other people con you into thinking that you should be doing for them what they are perfectly capable of doing for themselves. I keep a list of useful addresses, such as the local marriage guidance service, Relate (formerly known as the Marriage Guidance Council), but I would not contact them myself for another person. That is their responsibility.

In the list of selected books, I have mentioned *Games People Play*. If you read this with due regard to the counselling process, you will see several games which may be applicable. These include, "Why don't you?" "Yes, but . . ." This is a game which is characteristically played by people who want to demonstrate that their problem has no solution and to keep their counsellor seeking for answers, that is, to make the counsellor feel inadequate. They are getting negative strokes by giving the counsellor a put down. Do not fall into these traps.

If you are an astrologer and are counselling with the aid of the birth chart, there are some particular points to keep in mind. The first of these is that a birth chart is precisely what it says, something which is valid for the time of birth. Inevitably, your client will have refined this pattern by the time you see him or her. You do not want to get your first interview off to a bad start by telling the client that they are obstinate or quick-tempered if they have spent the last 30 years eradicating this fault.

There are two approaches which I have found helpful. For the first, I use the gentle art of euphemism and say, "You know your mind and don't change it easily", even if I mean, "You are obstinate". I can then go on to point out that firmness of character is admirable, provided the client knows when to unbend and become more adaptable.

This is also a useful approach in helping two people to see each other's points of view. A widow and her grown-up son, who were living in the same house, were not getting on too well together and she asked if I would analyse their birth charts. There is no doubt that he was an obstinate young man, but he also had the virtue that so often goes with it. He was absolutely reliable, a rock on which she could build. I pointed this out to her and received the reply, "I've always told John he was a pig-headed so-and-so, but you are quite right, you've made me realise that I do rely on him very much."

The other method is to emphasise to the client that you are dealing with a birth chart and ask whether he had certain traits, for example a quick temper, when he was a child. Sometimes, you will get the reply, "I still have" and you can go on from there, but in other cases the client will say that he has learned to control it. In either case, you have given no cause for offence.

Sometimes it happens that an astrologer, or any other type of counsellor, may get a client with whom they cannot establish a rapport. Since it is important that there should be a basic empathy between the two, it is better to tell the client straight away that you do not feel that you can help them and suggest someone who may.

I would like to conclude with an excerpt from *Astrological Counselling* by Christina Rose. Although, as the title suggests, the words are directed to astrologers they are equally true for any counsellor who wishes to go more deeply into the work than just trying to help friends.

> In the last analysis, effective counselling cannot be taught . . . It is a function which only through sustained practice (which may frequently be painful as the counsellor meets *her* limitations and blocks) enables her to acknowledge and accomodate the qualities emerging within her, which can foster an open participation with another person on his life's journey. Not all astrologers feel that they are suited to counselling. . . . Others are eminently suited to it. . . .

Each counsellor is the foundation upon which all of the knowledge or skills ultimately rest; therefore any training begins, and continues, *inside the person herself*. (The italics are mine.)

It follows from the above that training in counselling and the practice of it is invaluable in enabling the counsellor to become more fulfilled and at the same time, to help others to find fulfilment.

10
PREPARATIONS FOR HAPPY ENDINGS

One of the most frustrating periods in life may be experienced if you have a time of enforced leisure. While some people may welcome a chance to rest and follow an absorbing hobby while they are convalescing from an illness or are between employments others will be bored, restless and unable to motivate themselves.

This is something we should think about before it happens. It seems likely that there will be more leisure time for most of us in the future and we might as well use it to live more fully.

If you have read this far and felt that you were too old to start the process of self-development – think again. Grandma Moses took up painting at the age of 78 and enjoyed it for a further 23 years.

People are living so much longer, and in better health, that the old idea of 'three score years and ten' is no longer valid. By the year 2000, both the number of people over 60 and the number over 80 will have doubled as compared with 1970.

We should approach formal retirement, at age 60 we will say, as though we had 20 to 30 years expectancy of life. All of this time can be life-enhancing — a time to expand the mind, realise a few ambitions which need more leisure than we have had in the past and above all, a time to enjoy ourselves.

If you have 20 years or more ahead of you at age 70, at 60 perhaps another 30 odd, there is no excuse at all for not taking charge of the rest of your life. The World Health Organization has a motto, 'Add *Life* to years'. With a little forward planning, we can do just that.

This chapter is not just for the retired though. It is for those who are preparing for a major change in their role, or life script, in such a way that will enable them to take more complete control of their lives, making conscious progress towards self-fulfilment. This does not simply mean 'changing jobs', but creating space to do those things which have previously not been possible through lack of time or demanding commitments.

Time may be available as children cease to be dependent, or through shorter working hours, unemployment or redundancy. If the change is not welcome, it is even more important to plan for more free time. If possible, this should be done well before it occurs, so that the extra leisure or new work is eagerly anticipated and not viewed with apprehension.

Those who dread retirement or unemployment are the people who have identified so closely with their profession that they have only the one role (the life-script) and these are the ones who not only feel that they have no existence outside their work, but may actually cease to exist soon after that work ends. It is important that we should have plenty of activities and interests while we are employed, some of which can take more of our time when we have it to spare.

A great change in life-style always causes stress, but if it has been planned this can be minimised. People who have just retired, for example, need support, preferably from their family, but if not there are plenty of groups for retired people which will provide them with the companionship of their peers and new interests as they learn what others are doing.

There will be chances to eliminate unnecessary stress. Crowded trains will no longer be a daily hazard in getting to work and, unless you enjoy it, why drive your car in a large town where there is other transport available? The decision to let someone else take responsibility for getting you to your destination is one which could be beneficially made by many people judging by the tense expressions seen behind the driving wheel.

It is important to avoid taking on anything which can lead to a new stress, unless you want to do it. One of the pitfalls of having more free time is that other people can easily assume that it is at *their* disposal. You may be looking forward to seeing more of your family, but it is easy to drift into the role of the unpaid, permanent baby-sitter, shopper for all, etc. A way to avoid this is to have another engagement, but if you are already in charge of your life and have plenty of interests, you are less likely to be put into the position of having to refuse.

Ask yourself what you will most miss when you are no longer in full-time employment, and you will then know which is the most important gap to fill. For some people, especially those who live on their own, this may be the companionship of other people. If it is so for you, take up activities (before the event, if possible) where you will be likely to meet people with the same interests as yourself. We all need companions and it is important that we keep in touch — and I mean, physically in touch — the warmth of a handshake can be so comforting, hugs and kisses are life-enhancing. Don't be niggardly with yours; there is someone who would love to have such a response from you.

For some people, the most important gap might be the mental stimulation that they have had from their previous work. If this is your problem, you may be able to join a society which provides the opportunity of discussions on topics of mutual interest. If, however, your mental stimulus comes from working on your own, you might choose a course of study. You may also see an opportunity to become self-employed. Even if you have no wish to build a business empire and only want this activity to absorb part of your time, it can be rewarding psychologically as well as providing some income.

If self-employment is your aim, you cannot start making plans too soon. You need to identify a gap in the market for your talents. There is no point in battling to make a living with a product which is already too plentiful.

Then you need to plan for the capital and equipment you will need. You are more likely to be able to accumulate this while you are still earning and, as all commodities tend to get dearer, you will probably be able to buy equipment now much more cheaply than in the later years; but, of course, you must have room to house it.

Unless you really enjoy battling with tax and legal regulations, either consider getting a legal adviser or decide to do a job which you can do from home and which will remain small enough to cause no tax problems. There is no shortage of books on starting small businesses, or being self-employed. Read some of these first and you will soon see what is within your scope. In this, as in everything, you should set your own upper limit and stick to it. Remember, you are going to enjoy the rest of your life; leave time for your other activities. Plan to be busy and to keep occupied, but not to be rushed off your feet. The best self-employment is one which you enjoy doing so much that it ceases to matter whether you make money from it or not.

We have established that you need to keep mentally active and that you also need company. Some people will need this more frequently than others, but everyone should plan to be with other people on a regular basis. If you are self-sufficient and enjoy your own company, it can be fatally easy to become a recluse as you get older. The small effort of getting yourself ready to meet other people can become a burden if you let it, so make it part of your regular routine and it will become so habitual that you will never look on it as an effort. The third thing that you need is to get a change of scene sometimes. Apart from a short holiday occasionally, a day out quite frequently can be refreshing especially if it is undertaken in connection with one of your interests.

How can astrology help with all this? The moon sign and the position of the planet Jupiter in the birth chart will indicate the hobbies and pleasures which are likely to appeal. Jupiter is the planet of expansion, relaxation and pleasure, while the moon shows what activities will satisfy our emotional natures. Remember that you will have all the planets somewhere in your birth chart, so read through all the suggestions which follow.

LEISURE, PLEASURE AND THE ZODIAC

Aries would enjoy climbing or adventure holidays of the 'Outward Bound' type. As they get older, they might become leaders on this sort of activity for children. He or she would also make a good Scout or Guide captain. Days out need to be active. Sitting in a coach spells boredom to Aries, but they would probably enjoy ballooning. Exercise which co-ordinates mind and body is desirable. Mental activities will not be a difficulty, the Arien's mind is always active, but they need to find relaxing hobbies as well. Balance is the key to a happy leisure life for the Arien. 'All things in moderation' is a good motto for them and they should consciously slow down, though there is a need to pursue sports which represent a challenge.

Gardening and music are hobbies for **Taurus** and more leisure will give an opportunity to join the local horticultural society or herbal society. If the garden is not large, now is the time to consider renting an allotment and becoming self-sufficient in vegetables and fruit. A study course on interior decorating or architecture will provide plenty of opportunity for days out — National Trust properties, both houses and gardens, will hold much to interest the Taurean. They might like to take up painting, both attending classes and getting out into natural surroundings to pursue this hobby. As regards self-employment, they could become design advisers or financial consultants. They would also get a lot of satisfaction from familiarising themselves with the stock market and managing their own investments. Golf, swimming and dancing are all good exercise for them and they will be happiest if they structure their time, so that they get both mental and physical exercise and relaxation regularly. This is a good habit to develop, provided they do not feel that they must stick to it rigidly. One of the advantages of leisure is that one can do some things on the spur of the moment, because the weather is good or because a friend is free on that day.

Gemini will enjoy day coach trips to new places. They like travel and could turn their interests to good use by writing about them for holiday magazines, guide books, etc., or by organising parties for trips abroad. Their dexterity makes them good at 'do it yourself' jobs and they would make good demonstrators of gadgets or new products at exhibitions. Debating societies or public speaking classes will appeal to them mentally and they might consider going into political life, even if only at a local level. Sport such as fencing or bowls, both of which call for skill of hand and eye, will suit most Geminians, but they need to learn how to relax mentally and would get great benefit from yoga. They are often good conjurors and could find themselves in demand for children's parties.

If history has been an interest for **Cancer**, as it is for many of them, they would probably enjoy joining a Genealogical Society and tracing their own family histories. They might even start part-time self-employment by doing the same thing for other people. This activity will get them out and about and so will collecting antiques, which is also likely to be a Cancerian interest. Studying antiques or taking a cordon bleu cookery course need not be expensive, as some are run by local authorities as afternoon or evening classes. Most Cancerians like to entertain at home and some have flourishing businesses by catering for other people's parties. For exercise, team games, old-time-dancing and swimming are all excellent. The most important thing to remember is to have plenty to do. Be too busy to worry or brood.

Leo gets on well with children and activities with them will keep Leo young at heart. They shine as youth leaders, or in a drama group, perhaps producing plays with or for children. All creative activities make good use of Leo's talents and both males and females may enjoy making jewellery or pottery. Women may be interested in learning beauty therapy. This is another group who often enter politics. Exercise is likely to take the form of gymnastics or competitive sport. I am reluctant to suggest any self-employment for Leo, if they do undertake it, it should be part time only, or they will soon find themselves back in the rat race with all the worries that brings. Involvement in local activities, organising the hospital fete, for instance, would be preferable. In general, Leos need to avoid excessive expenditure of energy, mental or physical.

Activities which bring order out of chaos appeal to **Virgo**. They like repairing things, especially small objects like watches, and also enjoy jigsaws and mental puzzles. They are good at setting crosswords and could do this for the local paper or for magazines. Another hobby which appeals to them is stamp collecting. The local paper would probably welcome their contributions on matters of local interest and on literary or dramatic criticism. Voluntary social work is almost certain to be undertaken by the Virgoan with time to spare. They enjoy cooking with wholefoods and will exercise to keep healthy. Walking and swimming, together with specific exercises to keep them mobile, should be done regularly. In deciding what to do with their time, Virgoans need to make a conscious effort to do less work and not to drive themselves hard. Yes, they must keep busy, that is part of their natures, but they should vary their activities often, following physical exercises with mental stimulation.

Libra is likely to be the one who most feels the need for companionship and they should make the effort to visit friends who live at a distance as well as joining in some activity near home. Their outings might be visits to potteries or glass and porcelain manufacturers, and museums will have objects of beauty on show which are likely to appeal to their artistic sense. They need exercise each day and would enjoy team games, fencing and ice-skating. Mental activity is important and study on a subject which interests them could lead to self-employment as, for instance, an art historian. They are likely to undertake some form of social service, perhaps as a magistrate. The great difficulty for Librans with plenty of leisure time is to prevent themselves from getting lazy and then bored. This is such a waste of their life, since they have so much talent for happy relationships, if they keep themselves active.

There is no need to tell the **Scorpio** native to keep busy. Their difficulty is to stop themselves getting over-enthusiastic about their activities and not knowing when to relax. They are likely to enjoy such diverse things as potholing, doing voluntary service and studying psychology. Now they have leisure time, they need to find a creative hobby which relaxes the mind, as well as those which stimulate it. They might start to write detective stories, and follow a spell of this by listening to music, to unwind. They will enjoy activities with an element of risk, water skiing, diving, canoeing, boxing and karate, as well as the less demanding team games. Like their opposite sign, Taurus, they will enjoy looking after their own investments and may extend this to self-employment as a financial consultant. Research of all types is likely to attract them and, like Cancer, they would probably enjoy tracing the family tree. Advice to Scorpio — remember to rest, sometimes.

Sagittarius is another not short of activities, but they tackle them in a relaxed way. More leisure is a real gift to them, enabling them to pursue their many interests, which may well include attendance at race meetings or equestrian sports. Other day outings might include orienteering and rambling. Like Leo, they get on well with children and some Sagittarians interest themselves in organising sports for them and also for the physically handicapped. One Sagittarian known to me, helps them to build muscles by training them in weight-lifting. Many enjoy rugby football and golf, both with a strong social side. They must have a challenge, both mental and physical. Foreign languages represent just such a challenge and one they enjoy mastering, but their interests are so wide that many courses of study are open to them. Philosophy is a likely subject for their keen minds. Self-employment in retirement might include dog-breeding, translating, part time lecturing or writing. They love travel and good company and they tend to 'live it up'. They will have no difficulty in filling their leisure time, but they must learn to limit their love of rich food and drink, if they do not want to limit their lives.

The **Capricorn** native is most likely to be hit hard by enforced retirement, especially if they have achieved their ambitions within their careers and hold positions of power. It is particularly important to them to plan ahead for leisure, especially as they are likely to be long-lived. If it is possible for them to continue on a part-time basis as a consultant to their firm, this would be the type of self-employment they would prefer. They enjoy reading and collecting, but both are solitary hobbies and the Capricornian should have more social pursuits, otherwise they can easily get depressed. They will enjoy voluntary service and local politics. Days out can be spent in visiting ancient monuments and they would also enjoy archaeological digs, mountaineering and rock climbing. They should take part in athletic events, but these must be chosen carefully. Football is not a good choice as knee joints are vulnerable. Walking, swimming and dancing are all excellent for them. Music is often an absorbing hobby; not only listening, but also playing and composing. Like the Virgoan, their aim should be to keep their mobility and they must have congenial company.

Like Sagittarius, the other freedom lover, **Aquarius** often welcomes more leisure to 'do their own thing'. If they want to use an interest for some part-time employment, they might consider getting involved with local radio, reporting local news, or doing some research which will produce an article for the paper, or programme for the radio. The Aquarian has a gift for working with the mentally handicapped and this can be a good choice for voluntary work. Scientific societies and discussion groups appeal to them and may help them in perfecting their own inventions. Astrology and astronomy are naturals for them and if they decide to take up either, it will be a life-long interest. All open-air activities are good, especially cycling, and if the cost is not prohibitive, flying and gliding are usually enjoyed. Mental activities should be avoided late in the day; the Aquarian needs plenty of sleep.

The danger for **Pisces** with time to spare is that of slipping away into a dream world. Here are the TV addicts, who exist on fantasies, instead of really living. Now is the time to give substance to those day-dreams, *write* the novels, the plays, the poetry. Get them out of your head and on to paper. Get involved with dance-drama and choreograph the dances for the group. Study painting, antiques or other arts. Go swimming, sailing or ice-skating. Do voluntary work. This is all excellent advice for the Piscean, who will not need to be told to make time for reading or relaxing. Photography is often an interest for these people and then they could learn to develop their own films and join a photographic or cine society. In leisure or retirement, the Piscean needs to keep actively occupied, mentally and physically for some part of every day.

To these activities for each sign, I might add that all of them could study to become experts in their own subjects and then use their knowledge to give occasional lectures, or to teach at evening classes. The stimulation of imparting your own enthusiasm to a group of interested people, who will teach you even more by their own questions and observations, is a marvellous way of keeping the mind keen and your interest alive. At the same time it will take you out of the house and enable you to meet people.

We all need to come to terms with the fact of getting older but this does not mean limiting in our own minds the number of things which we can still do. It is a truism that the busy person is always the one who finds time to take on something else; the active man is the one who stays active longer. However, it is sensible not to use more energy than you need to accomplish anything.

Whatever our interests and talents may be, the process of moving towards self-fulfilment is a continuous and never ending one and it is particularly true that the journey is so much more important than arriving. With the right motivation, no matter what our position in life, no matter what our age and no matter what our faults and capabilities may be, the process of self-development, aided by the wisdom encompassed by astrology, can bring meaning and purpose into all our lives.

One final word to those who find it difficult to motivate themselves. You can only develop your willpower by using it.

Here are some suggestions made by Piero Ferrucci in his book, *What We May Be*.

> Do something you have never done before.
> Perform an act of courage.
> Say 'no' when it is right to say 'no', but easier to say 'yes'.
> When facing a minor choice choose without hesitation.
> Begin, at once, an action you would prefer to postpone.
> Break a habit.

Everything lives by what it feeds on. Give your will nourishment and it will grow. Let me leave you with the words of Walt Whitman.

> From this hour I ordain myself loos'd of limits and
> imaginary lines,
> Going where I list, my own master total and absolute . . .
> Gently, but with undeniable will, divesting myself of the
> holds that would hold me.

APPENDIX 1

ROBERT'S BIRTH CHART

This is the birth chart which is considered on pages 13 and 97. For those already familiar with astrology it will provide more background information to the text. For readers sending for a free personal birth chart (refer to page 159) it illustrates the basic constituents: signs of the zodiac displayed around the chart wheel; planetary glyphs positioned in the twelve houses (the Placidus house system is illustrated here); and planetary aspects — the lines joining planetary energies to show how they interrelate.

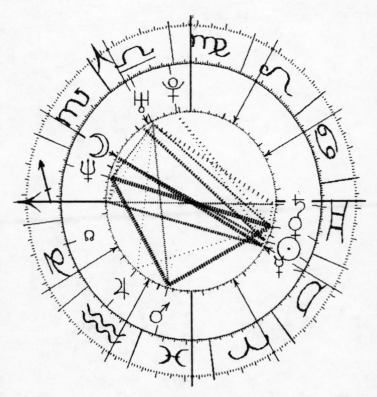

APPENDIX 2

RECOMMENDED READING AND CONTACT INFORMATION

Astrology

The Art of Astrology (textbook), Sheila Geddes, Aquarian Press
Synastry, Penny Thornton, Aquarian Press
Synastry — various, including Sheila Geddes, Astrological Association
Relating, Liz Greene, Aquarian Press
Star Signs for Lovers, Liz Greene, Arrow Books
Astrology and Health, Sheila Geddes, Aquarian Press
Astrological Counselling, Christina Rose, Aquarian Press
Wisdom in the Stars, Joan Hodgson, White Eagle Publishing Trust

Psychotherapy

I'm O.K. — You're O.K., Thomas Harris, Penguin Books
Games People Play, Eric Berne, MD, Andre Deutsch
What Do You Say After You Say "Hello"?, Eric Berne, MD, Bantam Books
Sex in Human Loving, Eric Berne, MD, Penguin Books
Encounter Groups, Carl R. Rogers, Allen Lane
Gestalt Therapy Now, Ed. Fagan and Shepherd, Harper Colophon Books
Gestalt Therapy Verbatim, Fredk. S. Perls, MD, PhD, Bantam Books
Transactional Analysis in Psychotherapy, Dr Eric Berne, Souvenir Press — Condor Books
Psychosynthesis, Roberto Assagioli, MD, Aquarian Press
Scripts People Live, Claude M. Steiner, Bantam Books
What We May Be, Piero Ferrucci, Aquarian Press

General-Psychological and Inspirational

Own Your Own Life, Richard G. Abell, MD, Bantam Books
The Farther Reaches of Human Nature, A.H. Maslow, Viking Press
Religions, Values and Peak Experiences, A.H. Maslow, Viking Press
The Wise Virgin, Annie Wilson, The Aquarian Press
The Psychology of Consciousness, Robt. E. Ornstein, Pelican Books
The Awakening Earth, Peter Russell, Routledge and Kegan Paul

Ephemerides and other tables

Raphael's Ephemeris (for any one year), published by W. Foulsham & Co. Ltd., Slough, Berks, England.

The American Ephemeris for the Twentieth Century 1900–2000 at Noon, by Neil F. Michelsen, Astro Computing Services

Tables of Houses for Northern Latitudes (0°–50° Lat. and Leningrad 59° 56' Lat.), W. Foulsham & Co. Ltd.

Tables of Houses for Great Britain. Lat. 50° 22'–59° North

Time Changes in the World, *Time Changes in the USA*, *Time Changes in Canada & Mexico*, by Doris Chase Doane, Professional Astrologers Inc.

(Note that *Time Changes in the World* does not include USA, Canada or Mexico.)

Periodicals

In the United Kingdom, *Prediction* and *Horoscope* are published monthly and are widely available from bookstalls. These will contain advertisements for astrological bookshops, services, etc.

Schools and Training

The Mayo School of Astrology, Alvana Gardens, Tregavethan, Truro, Cornwall TR4 9EN

The Faculty of Astrological Studies, BM7470, London WCIN 3XX

The Centre for Psychological Astrology, PO Box 890, London NW3 2JZ

Association

The Astrological Association of Great Britain, PO Box 39, North PDO, Nottingham NG5 5PD, publishes a journal and organises an annual conference, as well as numerous other events.

ASTROLOGICAL INDEX

YOUR FREE PERSONAL
BIRTH CHART

In owning this book, you are entitled to send its coupon to claim your free birth chart. Only one coupon per book will be accepted for the purpose of this offer. Photocopies of this coupon or any other representation of it will be ignored by the publishers. The publishers regret that they are not prepared to enter into correspondence on matters relating to this free birth chart. Safe receipt of the correct coupon containing **ALL** of the necessary information **AND** accompanied by a large stamped **ADDRESSED** envelope will guarantee our desptach of your birth chart. On no account may we be held responsible for any non-delivery by the postal services.

Additional birth charts may be obtained from the publishers at a cost of £4.99 each. Please write to *Self-Development With Astrology,* W. Foulsham & Co. Ltd., Yeovil Road, Slough, Berks SL1 4JH.

. . . . ✂

FREE BIRTH CHART COUPON

Complete and return with a large, stamped, self-addressed envelope to:

Self-Development With Astrology
W. Foulsham & Co. Ltd.
Yeovil Road, Slough
Berks SL1 4JH.

Please print clearly:

FULL NAME ....

ADDRESS ....

....

DATE OF BIRTH ⊔⊔⊔ ⊔⊔⊔ ⊔⊔⊔⊔
                           Day   Month   Year

PLACE OF BIRTH (nearest main town/country).........................

....

TIME OF BIRTH (state AM or PM) ....